MOVIES MAKE THE MAN

The Hollywood Guide to Life, Love, and Faith for Young Men

JEFF MINICK

ISBN: 1530623901
ISBN 13: 9781530623907

To my students

Acknowledgments

To those friends and family members who offered assistance and criticism, I am deeply grateful. I am particularly indebted to Miller Voigt for her insights and for the occasional "tap on the shoulder" and to Bonnie Gibson for her additional help on this book.

Table of Contents

Before The Lights Go Down: An Introduction   ix

Part I
The Difficulty Before Us
I Don't Wanna Grow Up: The Adolescent Man   3

Part II
Men Themselves
The Code   13

The Code: Part II   21

A Beautiful Mind   27

The Just and the Unjust   35

Sweat   43

Iron Men   49

Bad Boys   57

Transformers   65

Zuzu's Petals   71

Part III
Men and Women
Treat Her Like A Lady   81

Close Encounters of the First Kind   89

Chick Flicks: What We Can Learn   93

Sense and Sensitivity   99

Protect and Defend   105

Family Guys   111

Part IV

Men and God

The Hidden God   119

Faith of Our Fathers   123

Foxholes   131

Searchers and Sojourners   137

Part V

Character Is Destiny:

Mentoring, Males, and Motion Pictures

Men Making Men   147

Dangerous Waters   155

A Night at the Movies   161

Parting Notes

Appendix

Blast From The Past   169

Prompts For Discussion   173

Movies Make The Man: A List of the Films   175

Before The Lights Go Down: An Introduction

Although men of all ages—and even many women—may enjoy *Movies Make The Man*, I selected these movies and wrote this book with young men in mind, you who are between the ages of fifteen and twenty-five.

The movies I have selected for you meet several criteria. They are readily available from a store or an online company. Many are films still popular with viewers, and so should bring you pleasure as well as instruction.

Few action films— the Bond and Bourne movies and other such entertainments—appear here. Action movies are exciting and often teach commendable values, but in *Movies Make The Man* I have made realism of plot and character our priorities. Here you'll find movies about real men in real situations, men who face physical and moral challenges, who battle extraordinary enemies, who come to know in their bones, as a television sportscaster used to say, "the thrill of victory and the agony of defeat."

Bear in mind there are many other movies, many of them excellent, that teach lessons specific to men. Limiting the number of films here permits discussion of them in greater depth. Such deliberate limits also allow you to keep your rentals or purchases at a minimum.

In the back of my book you will find a list of the movies discussed here. Some are rated R. Some contain violence, sex, and profanity. If you're a younger viewer, you should preview, along with your parents, online reviews of these films.

These movies can provide a springboard for conversation between you and others in your life—parents, mentors, friends—who share in your struggle to attain the fullness of manhood. The idea is simple: you watch a selected movie together, then thrash out among yourselves its intentions and its relevance to your own life. If you need assistance driving such a conversation forward, you will find in the back of the book a list of questions designed to spark discussion.

And if you have no father, no mentor, no one with whom to share your thoughts and opinions about the movie? Let me suggest you allow my book to serve as a substitute. Watch the movie and then ask yourself: what does this film say to me about manhood? What does it tell me about growing into my proper estate? What lessons can I take from the story for use in my own life?

My chief hope for *Movies Make The Man* should by now be obvious: to inspire you in your quest for the full life, and to encourage you to seek out and practice the virtues and time-honored ideals of true manhood.

Part I

The Difficulty Before Us

Where do we get such men? They leave the ship and they do their job. Then they must find the speck lost somewhere on the sea. When they find it, they have to land on its pitching deck. Where do we find such men?

—Rear Admiral George Tarrant commenting
on carrier pilots in *The Bridges at Toko-Ri*

I Don't Wanna Grow Up: The Adolescent Man

Being a man is tough. Becoming a man is even tougher.

All around us we see adult males. Some of them are men. Others, despite being twenty-five, thirty, forty years old, remain adolescents.

An adult adolescent male is physically and legally a man. He has the voice of a man, the build of a man, the beard of a man. He can buy whiskey, join the Army, and make babies. He can do all these things and more, but he lacks the soul and spirit of manhood. He is psychologically and spiritually stunted.

Such half-men are readily identified. They often dress as they did in high school or college. Their love of amusement and toys—video games in particular—is little changed from the time they were twelve. These adult adolescents define commitment, ultimate commitment as in marriage and parenthood, as an obligation to be avoided. Duty is not a word in their vocabulary. Though many of them can work laboriously at a given task, they regard work as a hardship to be gotten around whenever possible. Frequently—and often unknowingly—they mistreat the women in their lives. Some of them have yet to grasp the notion that life is difficult, full of glitches, and they become frustrated and angry when their plans go awry or when reality cuts into their expectations.

Perhaps the deepest flaw in adult male adolescents, the flaw that serves as their trademark, is their glaring inability to put others ahead of themselves and their own desires. Like many teenagers, adult adolescent males focus their attention on their own cravings, blind to the wishes and needs of those around them. This selfishness in turn prohibits inner growth, that expansion of the spirit directing us to a deeper sense of our personhood and eventually to wisdom. An adult adolescent male may ski like a sixteen-year-old, but he cannot truly love a woman. He may know how to score big bucks on the market, but won't take time to play ball with his eight-year-old nephew. He works out regularly at the YMCA, but doesn't have a clue as to how a marriage works.

It would be convenient to hold adult adolescents responsible for their shortcomings, to blame them for their laziness, their blindness to the needs of others, their infatuation with themselves and their own interests. It would be convenient, but it would also be unjust, for our half-men are not solely responsible for their circumstances. They are not self-created nor do they suffer some genetic or gender deformity. No— these "men without chests", as C.S. Lewis once called them, these overgrown children devoted to entertainment and amusements, had plenty of help becoming who and what they are.

Boys have not always faced such difficulty becoming men. Not so long ago, they had to face tests of manhood—they fought in battle, hunted, went off into the world to find their own way, married, and built a family. For their examples of manhood they looked to those who had gone before them or whose achievements they had witnessed. These were the men they celebrated and emulated as heroes.

Such emulation—the study of a hero, whether by the glitter of a campfire or in the hush of a great library—inspired young men with the conscious desire to perform great deeds of their own.

Pericles' Athenians harked back to the golden warriors of the *Iliad* for inspiration in war and feats of arms. Patricians of Augustan Rome looked over their shoulders into the dim past of the Republic to take their measure of the ideal man. Knights of the Middle Ages found their standards for chivalric behavior and manly conduct in the legends of Beowulf, Roland, and King Arthur.

Until quite recently, many young men growing up in the United States also looked to the past when seeking models for imitation. The stoic leadership of George Washington, the philosophy of disinterest practiced by John Adams and Thomas Jefferson, the courtly manners of Robert E. Lee, the native wit and industriousness of men like Benjamin Franklin, Andrew Carnegie, Booker T. Washington, and Thomas Edison: these historical figures, their character, and their accomplishments served adolescents as models of excellence and high achievement.

Of course, these young men could also find such prototypes closer to home. Fathers, though often as flawed as history's great men, inspired and guided their sons. Here Theodore Roosevelt and Winston Churchill come to mind. Both men lost their fathers when young, yet retained for them a lifelong sense of great affection and gratitude. Churchill makes a particularly interesting study. His father maintained a distance from Winston, setting up a barrier formidable even for those formal Victorian times, and was often bitingly critical of his son. Yet in *My Early Life*, Churchill's 1930 autobiography, we discover a son enamored of his father, a young man whose deepest desire was to follow in his father's footsteps. (To read Churchill's stirring autobiography is to realize at once how much he studied men from the past as well as his contemporaries. Churchill was quick to copy those traits he considered worthy and virtuous.)

The last one hundred years have seen a tremendous shift in this practice of imitation. The captains of war, government, and industry who once served as templates of ambition and virtue for youth have given way to celebrities, music and motion picture stars, and athletes. Few young men today can name the achievements of warriors like Stonewall Jackson or Audie Murphy, of politicians like John F. Kennedy or Ronald Reagan, of scientists like Jonas Salk or Richard Feynman, yet many of these same young men can easily identify Brad Pitt, Jay-Z, or Kobe Bryant.

We have become cynical about greatness and great men. Our age, so promiscuous in its own relativism and sexual practices, looks down its nose at heroes, regarding no man as worthy of such a title unless he is perfect in every way. Washington and Jefferson fought for freedom from a British King, but owned slaves; Lincoln led the nation into a war that freed those slaves, yet was a melancholic; Edison was a brilliant inventor, but was a workaholic; Booker T. Washington was the president of Tuskegee Institute whose encouragement and efforts lifted up the former slaves of the American South, yet many now denigrate him as an Uncle Tom who should have pushed a more radical agenda.

Media has played a powerful part in promoting our worship of actors and ball players. Until the twentieth century, most entertainment depended on the efforts of an individual, that is to say, the participation of an individual. Reading, music, and games were the primary amusements of our ancestors, and these tended to be practiced by the individual rather than watched by an audience. The last century has seen this self-entertainment transformed into mass entertainment to so great an extent that we speak of the "entertainment industry."

This momentous shift toward mass entertainment has created today's larger-than-life movie stars, musicians, and athletes. Whereas even seventy or eighty years ago we might have found young men emulating the heroes from history books as well as athletes from neighborhood playing fields, many of today's young men are attracted to "stars" like Batman, Jason Bourne, and Michael Jordan.

Television shows and advertisements have further undercut manhood by setting men up as their punching bags, portraying them as stupid, naïve, sloppy, vicious, violent, or evil. Even a casual viewer would conclude from an evening's programming that men are too stupid to change a light bulb, much less manage a bank account, or else are so violent as to serve as walking commercials for universal male incarceration.

The textbooks and teaching in our schools have also contributed to this withering away of traditional heroes. History for the young is best approached through biography, through stories of real adventure, exertion, pain, and toil. Today's history books, however, focus on topics rather than on men and women—subjects like economics, politics, and social trends—which the young find dusty and confusing. Biographies available to the teacher these days have been watered down by political correctness and a tiptoe approach to sensitive issues. Some modern textbooks and biographies dwell more on Washington's slaves than on his leadership, on Theodore Roosevelt's imperialism than on his enormous enthusiasm for life and politics.

In the last thirty years, many schools have undercut traditional concepts of manhood by neglecting the needs of boys and young men. Rarely in our elementary and secondary schools are boys encouraged to be boys. A good number of school districts have shut down playgrounds or curtailed recess, and behavior once regarded as normal for adolescent boys—restlessness, a certain aggressiveness, a need for physical play—must now conform to feminist behavioral standards. Nor do most schools teach boys, or girls for that matter, to pursue the classical virtues: wisdom, temperance, courage, and justice. Young men discover these virtues, if they are discovered at all, in other places and often by happy accident—on the basketball court or the football field, in Scouting, in the Armed Services. The Marines, for example, seem particularly skilled at transforming boys into men.

In our universities, denigration of the masculine is endemic. Many universities offer courses and even majors in women's studies, while few, if any, teach matching courses in male studies (courses in which, as many universities well know, few men would enroll). Males have apparently sensed this hostility; in 2010, 58% of first-year college students were female. In some colleges this balance is so lopsided that college administrators are now recruiting males, offering them, as they have females and minorities in years past, preferential treatment. These administrators extend these incentives not because they give a tinker's damn about young men, but because the young women entering these schools are demanding more male companionship.

Churches, too, provide fewer male role models. Their largely saccharine take on Christ, God, and Heaven, their horizontal rather than vertical worship of God, their hand-holding and emotionalism: all are contrary to the beliefs and practices of most Christians only a century ago. This feminization of the pews has gotten so bad that a score or more of Christian authors, men and women, have recently published books on how to raise boys as Christians and how men can remain believers.

In addition, the diminished status of fatherhood in American society has reduced the male role models available to the young. Divorce rates in the last fifty years have skyrocketed, and though they have leveled off, these rates show little sign of descending, much less returning to the level of 1960. Less than half of all American children now live with both natural parents. More than 40% of all U.S. households are headed by single parents, 90% of them single women. (The United States leads the world in this statistic.) Among black families, 70% of pregnancies are to single mothers, and 70% of black children live in single-parent homes. White pregnancies outside of wedlock are about 40%.

These conditions often remove the father from family life, severing the bonds between a father and a son. Depending on circumstances, divorce can also create bitter enmity between a father and a son, leading the son to reject, on the basis of his father's actions, other models of manhood.

Procreation outside of marriage also cuts the father out of the family picture. This practice has become not only acceptable, but even fashionable. The beginning of the third millennium has seen an up-tick in favor of single motherhood. "I am woman, hear me roar," has made its way from the pop charts into the maternity ward. Some female movie stars, for example, have born children out of wedlock, their decision to do so celebrated by magazines and television. The young women who copy this behavior forget that those same movie stars make enough money to hire cooks and nannies.

Welfare and the federal government have lent a hand to this destruction of fatherhood and manliness. Senator Patrick Moynihan's "The Moynihan Report," a 1965 study in which he and others predicted that certain welfare policies would wreak havoc on poor, and primarily black, families, has long since passed from prophecy to reality. Our welfare rolls remain filled with young single mothers and not a father to be seen anywhere. The consequence for males? The same society that extends benefits to single mothers allows the fathers to remain in a state of permanent adolescence, bearing no burden for their children, no responsibility for the mother.

In addition to the various welfare programs for single mothers, the government has taken the place of the father in our society by offering all sorts of other give-away programs, ranging from easy loans for college to the latest revisions in health care. A system that allows twenty-five-year-olds to remain on their parents' health care plan clearly regards its citizens as juveniles needing band-aides and lollipops. We have shifted the financial obligations of fatherhood to the sugar daddies of the state and federal governments.

It is not my intention here to analyze these matters of manhood more deeply. Scholars with better credentials than my own have already delved into these issues. Those readers who wish to explore these topics in greater depth, who wish to learn more about the decline of manliness, the role of the hero in the lives of young men, and the increasing feminization of our society, may easily find such information through online searches.

Nor can I offer any far-reaching general solution to this problem—at least, not as it might affect the national scene. I have no grand plan for the restoration of fatherhood, no scheme to revive masculine virtues among the population at large, no lure to entice crowds of young men to read Plutarch's *Lives* or McCullough's *John Adams*. I lack the vision and the qualifications to undertake so large a task.

What I can do is show you some movies.

Part II
Men Themselves

Are we not men?

—Chant from Erle Kenton's
1932 film *Island of Lost Souls*

The Code

Men live by a code.

They may lack the skill to articulate that code. They may even be unaware that they live by a code.

But all men worthy of the name live by a code.

This code is a man's set of principles, often quite simple and plain, shaped from his breeding, background, education, and experience. A man's code is that set of rules which he cannot break without compromising his very soul. It is his Ten Commandments, his Constitution, the precious offering on the high altar of all that he holds real and good.

Living by this code is difficult—its tenets can bring disappointment, grief, hardship, and heartache. Temptation to follow the easy path lies at every crossroads, and each time a man bends or violates his code he feels within himself a little death.

A man can only endure so many little deaths, and then his self, his soul, the essence of all that he is, will die as well. This broken man becomes a zombie, a walking slab of flesh, a ghost of himself. This man falls into the ranks of what T.S. Eliot called "the hollow men."

Moviemakers have long recognized that men live and die by just such a code. Movies, after all, popularized the adage "the Code of the West." Even the tough guys of film noir—the detectives, the guys looking for the easy money, the crooks—follow a code. The heroes of action films obey an inner standard that dictates either success or failure, either a mission accomplished or an honorable death. From Clint Eastwood's *Dirty Harry* movies to John Wayne's Westerns, from *Die Hard* to *Air Force One*: in all such movies, the code dominates the hero, pushing him toward victory even when circumstances beat him down, giving him the strength to rise again from the ashes and follow his quest.

Not all of the codes produced by Hollywood are necessarily worthy of our emulation except, perhaps, in their root philosophy. Paul Newman in *Cool Hand Luke*, Clint Eastwood in nearly all his movies, Matt Damon in the "Bourne" series: these and many other actors portray that quintessential American type—the loner. We American males admire the loner, the outsider, the man who single-handedly rides into town and restores order. (A Texas Ranger was once sent to a town to quell a riot. "They only sent one of you?" the mayor said to the Ranger. "Well," the Ranger drawled, "there's only one riot, ain't there?") Our hearts are with the man against the crowd, the man who stands against popular prejudices, even sometimes with the man who, driven by injustice and fate, takes the law into his own hands.

Yet this code of solitary action as a standard of manhood can lead us down a dead-end street. If we are looking for models to copy, men worthy of emulation, then the loner, the action hero, and the hard guy fail the test. Can we see Cool Hand Luke as a husband and father? Can we picture Dirty Harry with a wife and family, the guy who mows the lawn on Saturday and takes out the trash on Sunday? Can we imagine Jason Bourne sitting around a barbeque, visiting with friends and sipping a beer?

These heroes live by a code, but it is the code of a loner. Like Huckleberry Finn, they are not boys, but they are not quite men either. They are stuck between adolescence and manhood. To study men who live by a code that works in the real world, men who live by values like responsibility, honor, and love, we need to look elsewhere in Hollywood for our examples.

Let's first turn to Sylvester Stallone's *Rocky* movies. Each of these six movies, with the exception of *Rocky V*, which was one of the worst movies of its decade, offers us insight into Rocky's principles. Many of these principles are as basic as the plots of the movies themselves: people judge you by your friends; fighters fight; the eye of the tiger is the eye of all great champions; families stick together; friends deserve our loyalty. Rocky's code, shopworn though it may be, offers men a way to live, to marry, to raise children, to endure annoying relatives, to make friends, to do well in a chosen profession.

Two examples of Rocky's code will suffice here. In the original *Rocky*, Rocky Balboa, a fighter who has never reached his potential, who is what his trainer calls "a bum," is going home one night when he spots a young girl he knows, Marie, hanging out with a gang of teenagers outside a bar. Rocky takes Marie away from these losers and walks her to her apartment. He knows that he himself is a loser, but he is also aware of the importance of reputation, the belief that what others think of us counts for a good deal in this world. He shares this insight with Marie:

"You get a bad rep, you understand, twenty years from now, twenty years from now, people are going to say 'You remember Little Marie?' 'No, who was she?' 'She's the little whore who used to hang out at the Atomic Hoagie Shop.' 'Oh, yeah, yeah, I remember her. Now I remember her.' See, they don't remember you, they remember the rep…You hang out with nice people, you get nice friends. You hang out with smart people, you get smart friends. You hang out with yo-yo people, you get yo-yo friends."

Though his words have little immediate impact on Marie—at her doorstep she shouts at him, "Screw you, Creepo!"—Rocky knows the truth of what he has told the young woman. He himself clearly grew up with yo-yo friends. What makes this moment with Marie all the sweeter is a scene in *Rocky Balboa*. One evening, Rocky returns to his old neighborhood and finds Marie working at a bar. Realizing that she has fallen on hard times, he reaches out to her, hires her to work at his restaurant, and befriends her son. By these acts of compassion, which spring from his code, Rocky teaches Marie that she can change her life.

In *Rocky Balboa* we arrive at the heart of Rocky's credo. Past his prime, his legs and wind gone, the former world champion nonetheless wants back in the ring for one more fight. The promoters of the new champion, Mason "The Line" Dixon, offer to put their man against Rocky in a bout for charity. After Rocky agrees to this arrangement, his son reproaches him one evening, furiously accusing Rocky of overshadowing his own life and efforts, and of making a fool of himself by his return to the ring. The son has a point: Rocky is old, and the odds are that Dixon will either play him for a fool during their bout or knock him through the ropes. Rocky reacts to this bitter criticism by telling his son how much he loved watching him grow up and how proud he is now of his accomplishments. Then he says:

"But somewhere along the line, you changed. You stopped being you. You let people stick a finger in your face and tell you you're no good. And when things got hard, you started looking for something to blame, like a big shadow. Let me tell you something you already know. The world ain't all sunshine and rainbows. It's a very mean and nasty place and I don't care how tough you are it will beat you to your knees and keep you there permanently if you let it. You, me, or nobody is gonna hit as hard as life. But it ain't about how hard ya hit. It's about how hard you can get hit and keep moving forward. How much you can take and keep moving forward. That's how winning is done! Now if you know what you're worth, then go out and get what you're worth. But you gotta be willing to take the hits, and not pointing fingers saying you ain't where you wanna be because of him, or her, or anybody! Cowards do that and that ain't you! You're better than that!"

This is Rocky's code: a man takes the punches life throws at him and keeps moving forward. Life throws many punches at Rocky, inside and outside the ring—the loss of his fortune, the death of a good friend, the death of his wife, the end of some of his dreams—but each time he falls he climbs again to his feet and keeps moving forward.

Secondhand Lions tells the story of a boy, Walter, being raised by two eccentric, wealthy uncles, Hub and Garth McCann. Like Rocky, Hub (Robert Duvall) openly shares his code of manhood. A former officer and hero of the French Foreign Legion, he lectures to wayward young men, giving them what he calls his "speech," the wisdom distilled from his own life on the meaning of manhood.

Secondhand Lions begins when Mae deposits her son Walter (Haley Joel Osment) at the run-down Texas ranch of the McCanns, whom she hasn't seen since she was a girl. Though unhappy about the arrangement, Hub and Garth agree to take in Walter for the summer while Mae attends secretarial school. (We later learn that Mae is lying to her uncles and to Walter; she has run off to Las Vegas to live with a gambler.)

Hub and Garth (Michael Caine) don't exactly greet Walter with open arms. As Garth says, "The last thing we need is some little sissy boy hanging around all summer." Slowly, however, the two men accept Walter and begin guiding him toward manhood. They share stories of their own youthful adventures and show Walter that, regardless of their advanced years, they still abide by a code whose core is honor and courage.

One scene in *Secondhand Lions* particularly demonstrates the idea that a real man is certain of his identity. When Hub and Garth stop along the road with their nephew for barbeque, some young punks enter the café. One of the punks accosts Hub, trying to take away a piece of his barbeque. When Hub shoves the punk's hand away, the younger man wants a fight.

Hood 1: Hey, who do you think you are, huh?

Garth: Just a dumb kid, Hub. Don't kill him.

Hub (to Garth): Right.

(Grabs Hood 1 by the throat)

Hub: I'm Hub McCann. I've fought in two World Wars and countless smaller ones on three continents. I led thousands of men into battle with everything from horses and swords to tanks and artillery. I've seen the headwaters of the Nile, and tribes of natives no white man had ever seen before. I've won and lost a dozen fortunes, killed many men, and loved only one woman with a passion a flea like you could never begin to understand. That's who I am. Now, go home, boy!

Once he has fought and trounced the young hood and his friends, Hub delivers his manhood lecture to them, afterwards declaring to Walter and Garth that the young men will be all right.

Later in the film, Hub realizes that Walter needs a piece of this lecture for young men. Here we gain a powerful insight into Hub's philosophy of manhood, a way of thinking whose bedrock principles reveals the heart of this aging lion. It is night, and Hub and Walter are standing by the pond on the farm. Because his mother has lied to him so many times, truth has become very important to Walter, and he demands that his uncle tell him the truth about Hub's own past. Were the stories he has heard about Hub's adventures in Europe and North Africa true? Had he really fought slave-traders, won a massive fortune by his wits, and married a beautiful woman named Jasmine? Hub stares straight into Walter's eyes and reminds him that some of the fictions by which good men live are more powerful than truth:

"Sometimes the things that may or may not be true are the things a man needs to believe in the most. That people are basically good; that honor, courage, and virtue mean everything; that power and money, money and power mean nothing; that good always triumphs over evil; and I want you to remember this, that love… true love never dies. You remember that, boy. You remember that. Doesn't matter if it's true or not. You see, a man should believe in those things, because those are the things worth believing in."

On first hearing these words in the film, many moviegoers misunderstand Hub's intent and may disagree with his argument. They contend that Hub is misleading the boy. We should only believe what is true, these critics say, otherwise we'll be living a lie. They are correct on the surface of the argument, but they are missing the point of Hub's lecture. Hub is not debating the value of truth—he has, in fact, lived out the tales told to Walter by his Uncle Garth. What Hub is offering Walter and other young men is a way to believe in "the things worth believing in." He understands that a code, a banner of honor, is sometimes irrational, that its values won't always match the values of the world, that a man can't always follow the easy path.

This code is the essence of a man. It is the basis of his character. And character, as observers from Heraclitus to Hollywood tell us, is destiny.

The Code: Part II

If we live by a highly principled code—remember that though all men may live by a code, not all codes are principled—then we are harder on ourselves than on others. We demand of ourselves what we are often willing to overlook or forgive in friends and coworkers. Moreover, all men will serve as leaders at some point in their lives, whether as a head of state or the head of a household. One mark of a true leader is the ability to suffer, to endure, to undergo pain and privation while still pushing ahead toward a goal, to keep our heads, as Kipling wrote in "If", when all about us are losing theirs.

In Wolfgang Petersen's *Das Boot*, the great sea classic of a German U-Boat and its crew, we witness an outstanding example of such leadership. Captain Lehmann-Willenbrock (Jurgen Prochnow) is a hard-nosed realist who runs a tight ship. Recognizing the necessity for such discipline and responding to the captain's concern for them, the men affectionately dub the captain Der Alte (the Old Man). Der Alte sets high standards for his men and knows the importance of discipline and command, but he also realizes the men need the opportunity to let off steam. In the captain's haggard face and weary voice we see the toll of leadership, the constant battle against disorder, against the unexpected, whether it be a Mediterranean squall or a British fighter plane. Like all good leaders, the captain prioritizes his duties and responsibilities: the safety of the ship is more important than any individual, the mission more important than personal comfort or opinion. The code by which the captain lives is not that of Nazism—he disdains Hitler's regime—but that of caring for his men, his ship, and their mission.

Sometimes Der Alte finds his code severely tested. During one attack by depth charges, Johann (Erwin Leder), who leads an engine room crew, cracks under pressure and fear, and deserts his post. By the rules of the sea, the captain has every right to have Johann shot where he stands, or to arrest him for cowardice in the face of the enemy. Eventually, however, and after mentally reviewing Johann's record—the man clearly knows his engines—the captain permits Johann to stay at his post. Compassion helps dictate this choice, but the captain also recognizes Johann's value to the submarine.

Ridley Scott's *Gladiator* provides us with another example of a leader who lives by a demanding code of honor. Like the commander of the U-Boat, General Maximus Decimus Meridius (Russell Crowe) is worn thin by his responsibilities directing the Roman legions against the Germanic tribes. Unlike Der Alte, however, Maximus believes in his cause and in his emperor, Marcus Aurelius (Richard Harris). After the emperor's son, Commodus (Joaquin Phoenix) murders the emperor, Maximus is forced into slavery, where he becomes a gladiator.

Yet Maximus never loses sight of the vision Marcus Aurelius held for Rome's future. Eventually, he fights his way via the gladiatorial contests all the way to Rome, where he hopes to revenge himself on Commodus, who has betrayed the dead emperor's desires for Rome and who had ordered the murder of Maximus's wife and son. After Maximus and his gladiators win a great victory in the arena, Commodus approaches him in front of the crowd, congratulates him, and then orders him to remove his masked helmet and to state his name. In this dramatic confrontation, Maximus takes off his helmet and turns to face Commodus, saying:

"My name is Maximus Decimus Meridius, commander of the army of the north, general of the Felix Legion, loyal servant to the true emperor, Marcus Aurelius,

father to a murdered son, husband to a murdered wife, and I will have my vengeance in this life or the next."

Notice here the hierarchy of loyalties professed by Maximus: his comrades, his emperor, his son, his wife. Here were his treasures, ranked by level of importance from the lowest to the highest. (When Maximus speaks, the shocked and sickened look on Joaquin Phoenix's face in this scene serve as one more reminder of this actor's fine talent.)

As Maximus gains a name for himself in Rome, we see that he has retained the loyalty of his former military comrades. Like Der Alte in *Das Boot*, he has shared their lot in the field, eating the same food, leading attacks, risking his life as they have risked theirs. During campaigns together Maximus had always taken pains to see that his men understood the dangers they faced. As a result, his men still love him and are willing to help him overthrow Commodus.

One hidden example of men following a code in *Gladiator* is the contrast between the code of the gladiator owner Proximus (Oliver Reed) and that of Maximus. Proximus believes the world to be "shadows and dust," in other words, that little we do here on this earth has any lasting consequence. (Even his name, hinting at the English words "proximate" and "approximately," underscores this approach to the world.) Maximus, on the other hand, believes our actions and words in this life count for something. As he says to his men before battle, "what we do in life echoes in eternity." As we see in the film, Proximus has lived most of his life following a moral code inferior to that held by Maximus, though his moral sensibilities do come alive at the end of the movie.

Another code embedded in *Gladiator* is stoicism, that ancient philosophy which recognized both the difficulties life can throw at us and the necessity of bearing those difficulties with equanimity. The real-life emperor Marcus Aurelius, himself a practitioner of stoicism, wrote *Meditations*, a book of reflections which remains in print today and which has served many generations as a guide to manly conduct. In several scenes,

Gladiator captures the stoic philosophy of endurance, courage, and the acceptance of life's conditions. Speaking to Commodus, for example, Maximus says, "I knew a man once who said, 'Death smiles at us all. All we can do is smile back.'"

The man to whom Maximus refers is, of course, the stoic Marcus Aurelius.

Stoicism as a philosophy is particularly useful to a soldier. In the opening battle against a Germanic tribe, Maximus and one of his subordinates bid each other farewell with the words "Strength and honor." This valediction is the cornerstone of their code, indeed, the code of all warriors.

In Daniel Petrie's *A Raisin in the Sun*, which is based on Lorraine Hansberry's award-winning play, we see male leadership on a smaller scale. In contrast to his wife, Ruth (Ruby Dee), Walter Lee Younger (Sidney Poitier) wants to become wealthy and goes to extraordinary lengths to gain what he considers his rightful place in the world. He wants to buy a liquor store, but is swindled out of the money. Meanwhile, his family has purchased a house in a white neighborhood. The neighbors want this black family out of their lives, and Walter, needing money, is tempted to sell the house at a profit to a man seeking to end the racial quarreling. Both Walter's wife and his mother Lena (Claudia McNeil) try to convince Walter not to sell the house, to follow a code of honor rather than one of mere profit.

Lena: Oh—so now it's life, money is life. Once upon a time freedom used to be life—now it's money.

Near the end of the movie, Walter takes up the reins of leadership. Having recognized the error of his ways, he changes direction to follow a path on which his family and his dignity come first. He makes a stand and keeps the house, which now serves as a symbol both for freedom and for the importance of family and heritage. When the neighbor comes to buy the house, Walter has become a man transformed:

Walter: We have decided to move into the house because my father—my father— he earned it for us brick by brick. We don't want to make no trouble for nobody or fight no causes, and we will try to be good neighbors. And that's all I got to say about that. We don't want your money.

After the neighbor leaves, Lena affirms Walter's decision by saying to Ruth: "He finally come into his manhood today, didn't he? Kind of like a rainbow after the rain."

Contrast the views of manhood in these movies with those of Stuart Rosenberg's *Cool Hand Luke,* mentioned earlier in our discussion on manly codes. Here Paul Newman brilliantly portrays an extreme outsider, that quintessential hero of twentieth century America. Luke is a man who cannot endure anyone telling him what to do or how to lead his life: not his superiors in the military, not the warden of the jail in which he is incarcerated, not even God himself, whom Luke addresses as Old Man. After being sentenced for two years to prison and a chain gang for cutting the heads off parking meters—he was drunk and bored—Luke gets into a fight with Dragline (George Kennedy), one of the biggest men in the prison. Time and again, the big man knocks Luke down, but Luke keeps getting to his feet until Dragline finally tires of beating him and becomes his friend.

After Luke's mother dies, he escapes from prison, is apprehended, sentenced to solitary, and finally has his spirit broken by the warden and his guards. Luke then makes one more defiant escape, and after being trapped in a country church, he is shot to death by one of the guards. Dragline, who has escaped with Luke, attacks this guard. When the movie ends, we see Dragline back on the road gang, chained at the ankles, cutting weeds with a swing blade, another Luke in the making.

Cool Hand Luke offers viewers an existential take on life. Luke exists through his code, which entails bucking up against all authority. Despite being presented as a noble character, however, and as a sort of leader, Luke does not offer a vision of manhood to which most of us would aspire. His rebellion when put into print seems somewhat silly. Certainly it is difficult, as stated earlier, to imagine him in any role in society—loyal worker, community leader, husband, or father. His broken relationships with his mother and brother, his failures with women, his assaults on authority: all make him less, not more, of a man. His values remain those of a rebellious adolescent.

Often rebellion and revolt are necessary for a man to keep his honor and dignity. Such rebellion marks many American films. We all enjoy watching Jack Nicholson take on Nurse Ratched in *One Flew Over the Cuckoo's Nest* or Kirk Douglas as a freedom-loving cowboy in *Lonely Are the Brave*. Such movies teach important lessons in independence, courage, and personal honor. They remind us that we too may be driven to take unpopular positions, that right and truth can exact their pound of flesh. Yet the heroes of these and many other films never quite grow into full manhood. Those who take lessons in manhood solely from such movies may thereafter find themselves following a code which not only separates them from close friendships or marriage, but which may even make them miserable and stunted as men.

A much more demanding master than rebellion is duty, that dusty, old medallion of the grownup world. The man who understands duty, who makes it a byword of his code, knows what he owes his wife, his family, his friends, his work, his God. Luke's words to Dragline—"Sometimes nothing is a real cool hand"—may play well to his fellow inmates and to some existentialists, but they mark the speaker as a man stuck in a pointless rebellion.

An integrated man, a whole man, a man of character, should understand how to take a stand when necessary, but he should also recognize, and try to fulfill, his obligations in life.

A Beautiful Mind

Man is made for thought and wonder. His mind and his senses combine to make him a creature of contemplation. To gaze with awe at the beauty of the world, to consider its ways and the ways of his fellow creatures, to ponder the philosophies of others, to construct a philosophy of his own: these abilities are granted to all of us, no matter how meager our intellectual capability. Enhanced by education, our capacity for contemplation, thought, and wonder is a distinguishing mark of the human being.

Some of you who are young may reject the training and education designed to lead you to these loftier thoughts. Sitting in a classroom, bored or bewildered, or both, you fail to see the connection between the study of logarithms or the sonnet, and your daily lives. If this is the case, if you don't understand that education leads us out of ourselves into a broader world—the word is derived from the Latin *educere*, to lead out—then you are setting yourself up for failure. You have become your own worst enemy. You are blasting away at your own potential, your own future.

Learning is often painful. It requires effort and determination. Recently, for example, I switched from a PC to a Mac. Because I am getting on in years, and because like so many others, I am disinclined to take on new challenges, this change was difficult for me. For several months

I had to force myself to go to the Mac and not the trusty old PC I had used for so many years. Finally I came to love the Mac, but as I say, making the shift was painful.

A dislike among young men for the classroom and learning is nothing new. In the old days, many of your ancestors preferred hunting or training for war to learning the rudiments of reading or mathematics. We have accounts of Alexander the Great stealing away from his tutors to ride horses. Similarly, many of you may prefer kicking a soccer ball or playing video games to learning higher mathematics, memorizing the names and facts behind the Battle of Gettysburg, or acquiring familiarity with the wisdom of Socrates, Aquinas, and Thomas Jefferson.

Many young men fail to comprehend that, like basketball or soccer, thinking requires exercise and struggle. The locker-room adage—"No pain, no gain"—applies to the mind as well as to the body. Learning and thinking, which are not always the same beast, can sometimes be painful, boring, or monotonous, just like exercise and drills in sports.

Many men prefer action to thinking. Even men with immense power, prepared by their education or experience to deal with disaster, will often advocate immediate action over thought or planning. The passage of the Stimulus Act in the spring of 2009 provides an excellent example of this preference for action. With the American economy smashed up on the jagged reefs of bad mortgages, foolish loans, and irregular practices in banks and on Wall Street, President Barack Obama, his advisers, and many senators and representatives told the country that something had to be done "now" to avert impending doom. If the Stimulus Bill wasn't passed "now," something "bad" would happen. These people never laid out before the country the precise nature of this disaster—nannies can't explain everything, after all—but whatever it was, our situation was bad, and we needed immediate solutions.

This demand for quick action by our politicians conquered reason, caution, and planning. Today, faced by a national debt of staggering proportions, we understand the dire results of such irrational haste.

To find a movie that celebrates reason in a man is difficult. Movies, after all, tell stories, and stories by their very nature require action. For every movie in which a hero conquers his problems with reason and deliberate consideration, there are a thousand in which the protagonist is an action-hero, a thinking hero, yes, but nonetheless a man of action beating back the bad guys with more brawn than brains.

There is, however, one magnificent film that shows us a man struggling with his conscience and trying his best to think his way out of the traps laid by his adversaries. Adapted from Robert Bolt's play, *A Man for All Seasons* tells the story of Sir Thomas More's struggles to preserve his faith and his life against King Henry VIII's demands for loyalty. More (Paul Scofield), a leading European thinker and a personal friend of the king, finds himself in deep trouble when Henry wishes to divorce his barren queen and marry his lover, Anne Boleyn. When the pope refuses to annul the marriage, Henry severs his ties with Rome, takes charge of the English church, and commands his subjects to recognize the legitimacy of his union with Anne.

More's friends and family counsel him, and eventually beg him, to concede the king's position and put his stamp of approval on the king's action. More, however, finds himself torn between his faith, which has condemned the divorce and the rupture caused by Henry's lust, and his family and friends, who want More alive and safe. Surrounded by enemies eager to break him, More seeks shelter in the bastion of wit, reason, and law. Here he discusses his situation with his son-in-law, William Roper (Corin Redgrave):

William Roper: So, now you give the Devil the benefit of law!

Sir Thomas More: Yes! What would you do? Cut a great road through the law to get after the Devil?

William Roper: Yes, I'd cut down every law in England to do that!

Sir Thomas More: Oh? And when the last law was down, and the Devil turned 'round on you, where would you hide, Roper, the laws all being flat? This country is planted thick with laws, from coast to coast, Man's laws, not God's! And if you cut them down—and you're just the man to do it—do you really think you could stand upright in the winds that would blow then? Yes, I'd give the Devil benefit of law, for my safety's sake!

Having cut his ties with Rome, Henry decrees that all must take an oath of loyalty to him as king and as head of the English church. In a conversation with Margaret (Susannah York), his daughter and a learned scholar in her own right, More lays out his response to the king's declaration:

Sir Thomas More: Listen, Meg, God made the angels to show Him splendor, as He made animals for innocence and plants for their simplicity. But Man He made to serve Him wittily, in the tangle of his mind. If He suffers us to come to such a case that there is no escaping, then we may stand to our tackle as best we can, and, yes, Meg, then we can clamor like champions, if we have the spittle for it. But it's God's part, not our own, to bring ourselves to such a pass. Our natural business lies in escaping. If I can take the oath, I will.

With each day bringing more demands and pressures from the king, it soon becomes apparent that More is trapped: he cannot recognize the king's actions as legitimate and there is no escaping the consequences. After being imprisoned in the Tower, and then tried for his refusal to take the oath, More is beheaded, an act which makes him a martyr in the eyes of the Catholic Church. Eventually, that same Church will declare him a saint.

Few other movies so winningly present the case for logic, thought, and conviction. More does not try to raise an army, lead a rebellion, escape his enemies, or evade the issue. Instead, he uses his mind like a rapier, parrying and warding off blow after blow until he is at last cornered and defeated. Each one who confronts him—the Duke of Norfolk, his wife, Margaret his daughter, William Roper, his enemies Thomas Crom-well and Richard Rich—reveals another side to More, illuminating his powers of reason and persuasion. Here, for instance, More is discussing his situation with his friend, the Duke of Norfolk (Nigel Davenport). The Duke, a bluff, hardnosed Englishman who prefers action to words, can't understand why More refuses to join the king and the vast majority of the clergy and nobility who stand with him:

The Duke of Norfolk: Oh, confound all this. I'm not a scholar, I don't know whether the marriage was lawful or not, but dammit, Thomas, look at these names! Why can't you do as I did and come with us, for fellowship?

Sir Thomas More: And when we die, and you are sent to heaven for doing your conscience, and I am sent to hell for doing mine, will you come with me, for fellowship?

We need men like Sir Thomas More, men who can see the long haul of things as well as the short race, men who don't join with others in a bad cause for the sake of fellowship.

A second movie in which men do battle by their wits is set in a courtroom. Sidney Lumet's classic *Twelve Angry Men* is the story of a young Hispanic on trial for his life for allegedly stabbing his father to death. The young man's alibi is weak, and several witnesses have placed him at the crime scene. The drama to this movie begins when the jury retires to its chambers. Eleven men quickly declare the accused youth guilty as charged. Only Juror #8, Mr. Davis (Henry Fonda), votes not guilty. His stance initially baffles, and soon infuriates, the other jurors. Here Juror #7 (Jack Warden) reacts to Wilson's vote:

Juror #8: I just want to talk.

Juror #7: Well, what's there to talk about? Eleven men in here think he's guilty. No one had to think about it twice except you.

Juror #10: I want to ask you something: do you believe his story?

Juror #8: I don't know whether I believe it or not—maybe I don't.

Juror #7: So how come you vote not guilty?

Juror #8: Well, there were eleven votes for guilty. It's not easy to raise my hand and send a boy off to die without talking about it first.

Juror #7: Well now, who says it's easy?

Juror #8: No one.

Juror #7: What, just because I voted fast? I honestly think the guy's guilty. Couldn't change my mind if you talked for a hundred years.

Juror #8: I'm not trying to change your mind. It's just that…we're talking about someone's life here. We can't decide it in five minutes. Supposing we're wrong?

Juror #7: Supposing we're wrong! Supposing this whole building should fall down on my head. You can suppose anything!

Juror #8: That's right.

As the arguments continue, the jurors reveal more and more of their interior selves, their prejudices, their characters, their virtues and vices. With emotions ranging from empathy to arrogance, they shout at one other and hurl insults as they debate the case. Despite the high feelings, however, it is cool reason that eventually prevails, reason that slowly wends its way into the argument, reason that, by means of this intellectual wrestling, trumps the passions and prejudices of the jurors.

George Gallo's little-known film *Local Color* offers another example of critical thinking. A young eighteen-year-old, John Talia, Jr. (Trevor

Morgan), has fallen in love with art and painting. When John realizes that an important artist, Nicholi Seroff (Armin Mueller-Stahl) is living in town, he visits Nicholi and persuades the elderly artist to mentor him, to teach him what he knows about painting. John goes with Nicholi to his Pennsylvania farm for the summer, where the Russian at first makes the young man perform hard labor while offering only a few tidbits about painting. (Think of *The Karate Kid* and Mr. Miagi: "Wax on, wax off.") Eventually, John learns lessons not only about art, but also about life.

Some of the best moments in *Local Color* occur during the intellectual give-and-take between Nicholi and his friend, Curtis Sunday (Ron Perlman), a critic and proponent of postmodernist art. Viewers aware of the conflicts in the art world between representational and abstract painting will be astounded by *Local Color*, for it drops down like a sledgehammer on the side of tradition and representational painting. During one of several heated dialogues, Nicholi and Curtis argue about the direction art has taken in the last century. Nicholi regards most modern art as pretentious and deliberately obscure; Curtis consigns representational art to the junk heap of history. When Nicholi asks Curtis's girlfriend what she thinks, Curtis cuts in, saying that she is a psychologist, not an art major.

Nicholi: I think it's madness.

Curtis: And what is that, my friend?

Nicholi: That you need a doctorate to appreciate painting. I mean, you don't need a diploma to appreciate music.

Curtis: Well, art has moved from what was once a communication to the masses, to what it is now, which is a communication to a far more select few.

Nicholi: And when did this happen? You are just as much a member of the masses as he, she, the farmer down the road.

Curtis (smirking): The farmer down the road has far different interests than you or I.

Nicholi: But art is a common ground. When you, Sandra, John, the farmer down the road take a pause for one moment and appreciate something that connects us all, it is the beauty of being alive, this art. Art that divides is not art.

A moment later, in the same discussion, Curtis attacks the idea of sentiment in art, calling it sloppy and sugary. Sentiment, he says, has no place in art. Here Nicholi responds fervently: "Sentiment is common decency. It is being a human being. It's knowing that life is short. It's very, very short...To cry, to hurt, to ponder, to love, to really love something. These are the building blocks of humanity."

With its obscenity-laden dialogue, *Local Color* will not appeal to everyone. Behind the old artist's vulgar language, however, stand truth and conviction. "The job of the artist is to uplift men's souls," say Nicholi, who sees trees as rooted men and angels hiding in the clouds. By the end of this film, we too begin to understand, whether we are painters or not, the importance of living a life in line with our ideals.

In our age of hasty thought, snap judgments, and instant communication, we need thoughtful men who are able to consider calmly the merits and deficits of an argument before rushing to judgment. We live in a culture in which speed has become a virtue and rudeness deemed a necessity, in which shouting and the brute force of personality beat down reason and nuanced argument. Many politicians and political commentators often argue more like children than adults, with insults and ad hominem attacks the order of the day. Our country needs men rather than boy-men to run its affairs.

We need, in short, men for all seasons.

The Just and the Unjust

Frequently men must deliver justice to those around them. Fathers break up fights between their children. Managers appraise the actions of certain employees and dispense justice accordingly. Lovers make assessments about their beloved. Because we all evaluate the other human beings in our lives, and then act according to those evaluations, all men are, in a sense, judges. The best of these men act with both justice and mercy in their dealings with others.

Justice is one of the four classical virtues, with wisdom, fortitude, and temperance being the other three. To the ancients, justice meant treating our neighbors fairly, weighing their actions with as little prejudice as possible, and acting with disinterest toward affairs in the community. Little practiced in our public arena today, this ideal of disinterest, which America's founders regarded as a the mark of a mature man, stresses thinking rather than feeling, acting impartially once the facts are laid out on the table, and putting the cause—whether that be winning a war or dealing with our siblings—ahead of our own desires and wishes. Thomas Jefferson intended high praise when he described George Washington and John Adams as men famed for practicing disinterest in public affairs.

This practice means removing, as much as possible, our emotions and prejudices from a problem while seeking a solution. Such impartiality is rare in our present age, where so many men and women elevate feelings over thought or attack difficulties with a bumper-sticker mentality. The man who takes up the practice of disinterest will immediately seem a font of statesmanship and discretion to those around him.

If you doubt me, try this experiment. The next time you become involved in a quarrel with a family member or friend, or in an argument over politics or religion, force yourself to step mentally away from the situation. Ask questions. I repeat: ask questions. Ask them sincerely and then listen—really listen—to what the other is saying. Look for understanding rather than making a rush to judgment. Then watch the reactions of the others involved.

Although many movies have dealt with this theme of justice—a large number of films are set in courtrooms, others involve civil rights of all kinds—few deal with the idea of disinterest, in part because we are so unused to the idea, in part because it sounds so dull. Of course such a philosophy needn't be dull at all. The most popular character of the first *Star Trek* series, for example, was Mr. Spock (Leonard Nimoy), who used logic to overcome obstacles tackled unsuccessfully by his human comrades. Swayed by emotions much less than the other characters, more intent on seeking solutions than on laying blame, Spock approaches problems in a disinterested manner.

Of course, Spock is only partly human; his father is a Vulcan. Since we are looking for real human characters to emulate, let's turn our attention to two mini-series: *Lonesome Dove* and *John Adams*.

Based on Larry McMurtry's best-selling novel, *Lonesome Dove* tells the story of a post-Civil War cattle drive from Texas to Montana. Heading up the drive are Augustus "Gus" McCrae (Robert Duvall) and Woodrow F. Call (Tommy Lee Jones), two aging ex-Texas Rangers off on one last grand adventure. With them is a band of assorted cowboys, some of them former Rangers like Joshua Deets (Danny Glover), others, like Newt Dobbs (Rick Schroder), who are new to the hardships of the trail.

Many lessons regarding manhood may be gleaned from *Lonesome Dove*. Gus's garrulous observations on women, the West, and life in general; Call's stoic acceptance of hardship and the flaws of men; the strengths and weaknesses the long drive brings out in all the cowboys: *Lonesome Dove* offers men young and old many venues for discussion and contemplation.

A key scene in terms of disinterested justice comes when Jake Spoon (Robert Urich), a ladies' man, card shark, and former Ranger, takes up with a gang of killers and thieves. Though Jake rides with these outlaws unwillingly—they have threatened to kill him if he tries to leave—he is nonetheless present when these men commit several acts of gruesome murder. Apprehended by Gus and Call, Jake, like the others, faces the rough justice of the rope. Though Gus and Call have affection for their former comrade, they make no exceptions for him. Gus says, "You know how it works, Jake. You ride with an outlaw, you die with an outlaw. I'm sorry you crossed the line."

Once the other three murderers have been hung, Jake, astride his horse and with a rope around his neck, looks at his executioners and says, "Well, hell, boys. I'd a damn sight rather be hung by friends than by a bunch of damn strangers…Well, adios, boys. Hope you won't hold it against me. Never meant no harm." Jake then digs his spurs into the flanks of his horse and executes himself, sparing Gus this harsh duty.

The difference between young Newt's grief at Jake's death—Jake is a hero to Newt and leaves the boy his horse before his death—and the hard justice of the older men is telling. Newt seems inclined to grant Jake mercy based on what he knows of Jake's personality; Gus and Call follow the stern path of justice. They recognize that whatever feelings they have for Jake must not supersede the just punishment Jake has brought on himself.

John Adams, perhaps the best American mini-series created in the first decade of the twenty-first century, vividly recreates the history of one of America's founders. Here we follow the life and struggles of John Adams (Paul Giamatti), the travails of his wife Abigail (Laura Linney), his fifty-year friendship, often troubled, with Thomas Jefferson (Stephen Dillane), and his working relationships with men like George Washington (David Morse). In addition to its lessons on judgment and disinterest, this television production, like *Lonesome Dove*, gives viewers many lessons on sacrifice, duty, and the meaning of personal honor.

Although this series depicts Adams as a passionate man (which he was), full of impatience and anger, viewers would do well to keep in mind that Thomas Jefferson himself, that great friend, and for a time, that great enemy of Adams, once said of John Adams that he was "as disinterested as the Being who made him." Jefferson recognized Adams as a man capable of putting duty and right before his personal desires.

The mini-series recognizes this idea. Realizing that Jefferson wields a mightier pen, Adams hands over the writing of the Declaration of Independence to the younger man. In another scene, set in the tense years just before the Revolution, Adams finds himself defending Captain Thomas Preston and his Redcoat troops, who shot and killed protesters during the Boston Massacre. His sympathies lie with the American cause, but his ideas of justice, of all men being treated fairly in a court of law, oblige him, as a matter of honor and right, to defend vigorously the men remanded to his charge. His cousin, Sam Adams, admonishes him for taking up their cause.

Sam: You haven't much of a case, John.

John: Have I not?

Sam: No Boston jury will vote for acquittal.

John: Thank you for your kind advice, Sam.

Sam: This is not a time for showing how clever you are, cousin. This is a time for choosing sides.

John: I am for the law, cousin. Is there another side?

Sam: There are those who would fight for our rights as natural-born Englishmen, and those that would strip us of those rights!

John: I do not have the luxury of your birth or your purse, Sam, to spend my days fomenting dissension.

John (calling out to Sam as he leaves): I intend to prove this colony is governed by law. Whatever you or your Sons of Liberty may say on the matter!

Adams won the case.

Sometimes our worst failures in the realm of assessment come not from the evaluation of other men or causes, but in the scrutiny of our own morality. To one extent or another, all men pursue the paths of self-interest, seeking goods and benefits for their own advancements and pleasures. Even a less than noble motive for this pursuit may still prove beneficial to the pursuer and those around him. The twenty-year-old lured into medicine by a love for science and big bucks may lack the bed-side skills of his counterparts, but he may nonetheless save lives while finding satisfaction in his large house and thick financial portfolio.

The difficulty arises when we begin lying to ourselves, when we put aside the critical faculties allowing for self-evaluation. Blind and deaf to all but our own wishes and dreams, we soon find ourselves reverting to adolescent behavior and selfish thoughts. We no longer see from a mountaintop. Instead, we have wandered into a mist-covered valley in which the only reality is the self. This failure of good sense and personal examination may have profound consequences for the man who finds himself in such a place.

Robert Redford's *Quiz Show* takes us into the heart and soul of a man betrayed by his own ego. Here Charles Van Doren (Ralph Fiennes), an associate professor at Columbia and the son of famed poet and professor Mark Van Doren (Paul Scofield), is enticed onto a 1950s television game show where cheating—certain candidates are given the answers before the show—is endemic. At first, Charlie resists the offer to cheat, to take the answers ahead of time, but the fame and money soon prove too much for his personal scruples. Greed overcomes rectitude, and Charlie tosses away his standards of fair play and integrity.

After the Justice Department investigates the growing scandal, attorney Dick Goodwin (Rob Morrow) confronts Charlie to ask whether he was given the answers to the questions while on the show. Charlie wiggles away from this interrogation and only reveals the truth about the show when ordered to appear before a Congressional committee investigating corruption in television. There he delivers a polished statement in which he admits his guilt while at the same time pleading for mercy and understanding. Most of those on the committee appear sympathetic to his explanation of how he fell prey to scandal, and they applaud him for his forthrightness. Then Congressman Derounian (Joseph Attanasio) interrupts with a chilly reminder: "I'm happy you have made the statement. But I cannot agree with most of my colleagues. See, I don't think an adult of your intelligence should be commended for simply, at long last, telling the truth."

Quiz Show takes us on a tour of the slippery slope leading to corruption. The television director and producer first slip Charlie questions they know he can answer. Then, after a debate with them and with himself, Charles agrees to take the questions before the show so that he might research the answers on his own. Finally, the façade of honesty crumbles completely, and he accepts the answers outright.

Quiz Show examines in meticulous detail how easily and smoothly Charles Van Doren's slow moral ruination proceeds, just as it may proceed for many of us. Step by step, Charlie gives up his ideals regarding truth and honor, using the excuse that "it's just television."

We also gain a fine lesson from *Quiz Show* about the connection between our name and our honor. In a scene set in an empty college classroom, Charlie goes to his father for advice. Knowing now that the Justice Department will investigate him, he confesses his misdeeds, then ranges in his explanations for his moral collapse from self-pity to self-righteous anger. When his father upbraids him, Charlie says the matter shouldn't affect his father, that only his own reputation and name are at stake. In one of the most telling lines of the movie, his father roars back at him: "Your name is mine!"

This is a shocking scene. Those four words remind the audience what is often forgotten today: our names matter. Our reputations matter. In the eyes of other men, our name embodies our reputation. Whether we lie to a friend or make ourselves ridiculous through photographs on Facebook, we need to be aware that men of integrity are watching and judging our own lack of judgment.

Our practice of disinterest may draw the criticism of others, but at least we can look ourselves in the mirror the next morning.

Sweat

You shall earn your bread by the sweat of your brow, the Old Book says, and the majority of men still live by this maxim. They farm the land and fish the seas. They build great buildings. They craft fine furniture by hand and manufacture automobiles on assembly lines. They push brooms and drive heavy machinery. They are plumbers, electricians, and carpenters, insurance salesman and bank managers, mechanics and cab drivers.

Because some professions lend themselves readily to film and because writers and directors are comfortable portraying these professions on the big screen, Hollywood tends to be limited and formulaic in its matching of film heroes and the work they do. Who has not seen a movie about soldiers and their training and their battles? About lawyers fighting in a courtroom or doctors waging war on death in a hospital? Writers, artists, teachers, ball-players, policemen, detectives, politicians: these are some other popular professions featured in film.

On the other hand, how many of us can remember a movie in which the protagonist is a plumber who demonstrates the level of his skills? How many movies tell the story of a carpenter who uses all his gifts and talents to keep his wife and children fed? How many movies ever show us a skilled auto mechanic working in his shop as a background to some more dramatic story?

Our society tends to disdain those who work with their hands. Doctors, lawyers, soldiers, poets: these are the men, we are told, who lead adventurous lives. The guy with engine oil under his fingernails, the guy who crawls under a house in January to repair a burst pipe, the guy who knocks himself out working in a brewery by day and then goes home to farm a garden in the evening: these men are rarely the subject of movies.

And if they do happen to come to the attention of Hollywood's writers, such men are often depicted as hating their jobs. If you Google "movies about work," you will find nearly all the films stress the negative side of work. Other films portray blue-collar workers as boozing, bitter, wife-beating rednecks too stupid for office work. Such movies typically feature as a protagonist the worker's son, usually a sensitive boy who wants nothing more than to escape his father's life of drudgery and so runs away to the city to discover his real talent.

It is unfortunate for young men that Hollywood, and our society at large, devalue such labor, that we regard so many necessary jobs as demeaning, that those who work with their hands are somehow inferior to those who work at a desk. *Good Will Hunting*, for example, presents us with four young Boston men, all of them working day-labor jobs. Will Hunting (Matt Damon) is employed as a janitor at a university who is inexplicably blessed with high intelligence and a photographic memory. By way of these intellectual gifts, Will eventually escapes his low-class job and his ramshackle life. His friends are left behind, clearly fated to follow lives of crummy jobs, street fights, boozing, and broken dreams.

If we actually look at the working class in America, at the people who keep our society moving, who pay their bills and taxes, we find that many of these men don't lead such dull or depressing lives. Over time, many of them increase their skills and pay levels, buy homes, and invest their money for the future. They marry well and raise children, and are often just as happy as anyone else on the planet.

Such men, moreover, are necessary to our way of life. They are important to us. Who does not admire a skilled craftsman? Who does not treasure the clever handyman who can fix everything from a leaky faucet to leaky roof? What would we do without such men?

Even less common than movies with a craftsman as the protagonist are movies examining the meaning of work and the work ethic. We've all seen movies, documentaries, and television shows set in hospitals, courtrooms, gymnasiums, artists' studios, spacecraft, and police stations, yet even these movies rarely present a philosophy of work, an ethic of work that should be part of the bone and nerve of the real man. If movies do address the philosophy of work, they often depict physical labor as something we should avoid whenever possible. Work is a burden, a prison cell to which we are condemned. Rare indeed is the movie offering us a philosophy of work, that explores the proper relationship between what we produce and who we are.

King Vidor's *The Fountainhead* is one of these rarities. Ayn Rand, heroine to many libertarians for her passionate writings on the individual versus the state, composed both the novel and the film script, and the movie therefore may be taken as an account of her ideas. We don't have to agree with those ideas to see that *The Fountainhead* takes a vital interest in the meaning of work. The entire movie, in fact, is about work and creativity, their value, and their relation to the human person.

The Fountainhead, justly described by several reviewers as "camp," tells the story of Howard Roark (Gary Cooper), an architect who respects only individual vision and craft. Dominique Francon (Patricia Neal) briefly becomes Roark's lover, but then marries the rich and powerful Gail Wynand (Raymond Massey), the publisher of "The Banner," a New York newspaper. In the meantime, Peter Keating (Kent Smith) asks Roark to help design Cortlandt Homes, a low-cost housing development. Roark agrees, but stipulates that his plans must be followed exactly.

Roark lays out the building on paper, but when he discovers that others have altered his building plans, an embittered Roark dynamites the project and then faces trial for the damage he has done. Arrested for his crime, Roark suffers blistering attacks from "The Banner" and other newspapers for daring to stand apart from humanity and for his unique vision in the building trade. After a long and stirring speech in which he declares that "My reward, my purpose, my life is the work itself—my work done my way! Nothing else matters to me," Roark wins acquittal from a sympathetic jury. Acknowledging the errors he made in criticizing Roark, Wynand asks the architect to raise a skyscraper of his own design as a memorial and then kills himself, leaving Dominique and Roark to marry.

The Fountainhead must answer guilty to charges of over-dramatization (Rand loved the exclamation point), silly lines, and histrionic speeches. At the same time, however, it is one of the few major American films that actually discusses at length and with some intelligence the place of work and creativity in our lives. In his speech at his trial, for example, Howard Roark says:

"Our country, the noblest country in the history of men, was based on the principle of individualism. The principle of man's inalienable rights. It was a country where a man was free to seek his own happiness, to gain and produce, not to give up and renounce. To prosper, not to starve. To achieve, not to plunder. To hold as his highest possession a sense of his personal value. And as his highest virtue, his self respect. Look at the results. That is what the collectivists are now asking you to destroy, as much as the earth has been destroyed."

One film that does celebrate the skills of the workingman is *Lilies of the Field*, the story of an ex GI driving across the western United States seeking construction work. Homer Smith (Sidney Poitier) encounters five nuns trying to build a church and school for a community in the desert. Homer, a handyman and builder, performs several repair jobs for the nuns, at which point Mother Maria (Lilia Skala) cajoles him into building a chapel. Mother Maria is a demanding taskmaster, and she and Homer are at loggerheads throughout the film. At one point, when Mother Maria is calling on him for more work and advice, a weary Homer responds with a joke at his treatment so far:

Mother Maria: Schmidt! Schmidt!

Homer Smith: Old Mother gonna feed the slaves?

Lilies of the Field is a celebration of men like Homer Smith. The nuns value him for his humor and goodhearted philosophy, true, but they also understand his value as a worker. They, and we, see the skills Homer brings to his work.

Some movies do give us insights into the intricacies of a man's work without calling attention to that work, that is, the daily occupation of the man serves as a backdrop to the action on the screen. One of the finest of these films is Lasse Hallstrom's *An Unfinished Life*. Einar Gilkyson (Robert Redford) is an aging Wyoming rancher who is taking care of a friend and fellow rancher, Mitch (Morgan Freeman), the victim of a bear attack. Then Jean Gilkyson (Jennifer Lopez), his estranged daughter-in-law whom Einar holds responsible for his son's death in a car accident, shows up at the ranch on the run from an abusive boyfriend. Her presence reopens Einar's wounds of grief and loss, and he finds himself torn by emotions: anger over his lost son, harsh resentment toward Jean, and a growing affection for the grand-daughter he has never known.

Throughout *An Unfinished Life,* Hallstrom shows rather than tells us what life on a working ranch holds for Einar. He works daily on the property, performs his own repairs on his truck, and spends much of his time in the early mornings and late evenings caring for Mitch. We become familiar with a man whose work—grinding, relentless, and sometimes dangerous—is central to his entire life. In Redford's grizzled face is the history of a man, a rancher who rises every morning before dawn and who spends long hours working with his hands and his mind.

As you move into the labor force, in whatever capacity, you must remember the importance and dignity of work not only in your own life, but also in the lives of those around you. Once young men your age would have acquired that knowledge by direct observation and participation, by working on the family farm, by hiring themselves out even when teenagers and contributing their earnings to the family income. For many of you today, whether you are raised in an inner city where few jobs exist or in a suburb where by dint of the family's status you escape the household chores once the domain of your grandfathers, work may become a foreign territory, a circumstance viewed as interfering with pleasure, which so many men now regard as their chief purpose in life.

Parents and mentors should help you become aware not only of the necessity of work, but of the ultimate part work plays in shaping the dignity of a man and his purpose in life. Here movies are only a partial help.

In the case of work, experience—mowing the lawn, caring for the house or apartment, a summer job—truly is the best teacher.

Iron Men

*R*ocky. *Rudy. Raging Bull. Brian's Song. Miracle. Angels in the Out-field. Mighty Ducks. Pride of the Yankees.* The list of movies about athletes and sports could go on and on.

Given the popularity and number of these films, we viewers clearly love stories about sports, stories where the athlete battles and overcomes personal difficulties, defeats a worthy opponent, wins the championship game, and leaves the field waving a trophy. These feel-good movies allow us to experience vicariously what the television show Wide World of Sports once trumpeted as "the thrill of victory and the agony of defeat."

Most of these movies tell us that such victories come with a cost, a price to be stamped paid by those who pursue victory and the winner's circle. By studying this cost, we can learn additional lessons about manhood and the virtue of fortitude. The sacrifices, grit, and willpower of the playing field can be the seed, water, and sun that produce real men.

In David Anspaugh's *Hoosiers*, Coach Norman Dale (Gene Hackman) arrives in a small Indiana town to teach civics and coach basketball at the local high school. Though he once coached college ball, Dale left in disgrace after losing his temper and hitting one of his players. Coaching this high school team offers Dale his last chance at redemption in the sport he loves.

From the moment he puts on his coach's whistle, Dale rouses the anger of some of the townspeople, who want their players to win games by their customary run-and-gun shooting. Coach has something else in mind. To his players he says, "I've seen you guys can shoot, but there's more to the game than shooting. There's fundamentals and defense."

Coach Dale also manages to tick off Myra Fleener (Barbara Hershey), a teacher in the same school. Disgusted by the importance the town attaches to basketball, Myra is afraid the Coach will try to lure loner and former player Jimmy (Marius Valainis) back onto the court, thereby hurting the young man's chances for an academic scholarship.

Myra: You know, a basketball hero around here is treated like a god. How can he ever find out what he can really do? I don't want this to be the high point of his life. I've seen them, the real sad ones. They sit around the rest of their lives talking about the glory days when they were seventeen years old.

Norman Dale: You know, most people would kill to be treated like a god, just for a few moments.

Upset with the coach's training techniques and some losses on the court, the school board is on the verge of firing Coach Dale when Jimmy makes a surprise appearance at the meeting. He promises to play basketball, but yokes that promise to a demand: Norman Dale must be retained as coach. Jimmy, who has secretly observed Coach Dale, understands his dreams for the players and recognizes in him the qualities of grit and fire needed by the team.

At one point in *Hoosiers*, Dale says what all great coaches believe, what all young men need to hear—not just once, but again and again: "If you put your effort and concentration into playing to your potential, to be the best that you can be, I don't care what the scoreboard says at the end of the game. In my book we're going to be winners."

By the end of *Hoosiers*, the boys on the team have taken a giant step into manhood. They have welded themselves into a team, not a gang of individual shooters, and have realized a dream larger than their individual selves.

Coach Dale has also grown as a man. Although he retains the intensity that he carried into the school, his love for his players has taken the rough edges off his temper, and he makes amends for his past mistakes.

Most sports movies depict young men engaged in conflict both on and off the field. Like *Hoosiers*, *Remember The Titans* is based on a true story. The time is 1971, and two Northern Virginia high schools—one with white students, the other with black—must end their segregation and integrate their programs. The football players who gather for summer training are the first students to encounter the practical difficulties of this desegregation. The white coach, Bill Yoast (Will Patton), must give up his post as head coach to a black man, Coach Herman Boone (Denzel Washington), newly arrived from North Carolina.

At first, tensions run high in training. Fights break out between black and white players; the players don't function as a team; the coaches are unhappy. In an effort to ease this friction, Coaches Boone and Yoast take their players to a training camp near Gettysburg, Pennsylvania. Forced by these men to learn as much as possible about one another, and drilled hard in football every day, the players slowly coalesce into a team. One key scene takes place in the team cafeteria, when Lewis, a white easy-going lineman, sits at a table with his black teammates:

Julius: What you doin' man?

Lewis: Eatin' lunch.

Julius: I see you eatin' lunch, but why ain't you eatin' over there? Why not go over there and eat with your people?

Lewis: Man, I don't have any people. I'm with everybody, Julius.

Petey: Yeah, he's just a light-skinned brother.

Julius: (laughs)

Petey: Come on Julius, he's just another blessed child in God's lovin' family.

The characters who grow most in this movie are Gerry Bertier (Ryan Hurst), the white team captain, and his co-captain, black team-mate Julius Campbell (Wood Harris). Enemies at first, they overcome their bigotry and dislike for each other at the training camp. Eventually, both young men become friends, breaking up racial altercations at school, visiting each other's homes, and hanging out together on the weekends. After a car accident leaves Gerry Bertier paralyzed and in the hospital, both young men realize the depths of their friendship.

Nurse to Julius: Only kin's allowed in here.

Gerry: Alice, are you blind? Don't you see the family resemblance? That's my brother.

Then, when Gerry becomes aware of Julius staring at him, they awkwardly express their affection:

Gerry: Well, you think I look banged up, you should see my Camaro.

Julius: Man, I sure am sorry, man. I should have been there with you.

Gerry: What are you talking about? You would've been in that bed right next to me.

Julius: You can't be hurt like this. You—you're Superman.

Gerry: I was afraid of you, Julius. I only saw what I was afraid of, and now I know I was only hating my brother.

Julius: I'll tell you what, though. Um, when all this is over...me and you are gonna move out to the same neighborhood together. OK? And, um...and we'll get old, and we'll get fat. And there ain't gonna be all this black-white between us.

Gerry (chuckles): Left side.

Julius: Strong side.

In one of their toughest games, Julius shows his coaches he has absorbed their teachings—not only the lessons that make a great athlete, but also those that make a great man.

Coach Boone: It's all right. We're in a fight. You boys are doing all that you can do. Anyone can see that. Win or lose...We're gonna walk out of the stadium tonight with our heads held high. Do your best. That's all anyone can ask for.

Julius: No, it ain't, Coach. With all due respect, you demanded more of us. You demanded perfection. Now, I ain't saying that I'm perfect, cause I'm not. And I ain't gonna never be. None of us are. But we have won every single game we have played until now. So this team is perfect. We stepped out on that field that way tonight. And if it's all the same to you, Coach Boone, that's how we want to leave it.

Coach Yoast: Yeah. I hope you boys have learned as much from me this year as I've learned from you. You've taught this city how to trust the soul of a man rather than the look of him. And I guess it's about time I joined the club.

Julius has gained an important lesson from his coaches and the game he plays. He has learned to strive to do better than his best, to squeeze out sweat and blood beyond any effort he has ever made.

Remember The Titans drums home this lesson: hard work, training, and desire pay off. It also reminds these young athletes—and the rest of us—that great and noble goals are often achieved with teamwork and planning.

In Sylvester Stallone's *Rocky II*, Rocky (Sylvester Stallone), promises his newly wed wife Adrian (Talia Shire) to give up boxing after losing to the champion Apollo Creed (Carl Weathers). For a while he flounders around looking for other work, preferably in an office. After several failures—the fighter, for example, too inarticulate to deliver the lines in the script, flubs a commercial for which he has been hired—Rocky receives a lesson in life from the manager of an employment agency:

Manager: Can I be honest? No one's going to offer you an office job. There's too much competition. Why don't you fight? I read somewhere that you are a very good fighter.

Rocky: Yeah, well. Was you ever punched in the face 500 times a night? It stings after a while, you know.

The employer recognizes Rocky's natural talent, and soon the fighter follows the man's advice. He realizes that he is not only good at fighting, but that boxing is his vocation, his calling in life. He schedules a rematch with world champion Apollo Creed (Carl Weathers) and begins training.

Rocky's pregnant wife Adrian (Talia Shire) opposes this decision, certain that Rocky will be injured in the ring. Her silent opposition lowers Rocky's morale and damages his training efforts. Something goes wrong when the baby is born, and Adrian falls into a coma. Though he should be training for the big fight, Rocky stays by her bed or in the hospital chapel, praying, reading to her, talking to her, and rebuffing his trainer's efforts to get him to the gym for practice. Eventually, Adrian awakes, and Rocky rejoices. She then pulls him close, and whispers:

Adrian: There's one thing I want you to do for me.

Rocky: What's that?

Adrian: Win...Win!

Elated by her support, Rocky returns to the gym and training for his upcoming match with Apollo Creed.

Rocky is one of the lucky men on this planet. Not only does he have the support of a good woman, but he also recognizes his calling, his vocation. He knows why he is here. "Fighters fight," he says, and Rocky Balboa is a fighter. He is gifted with a talent and, more importantly, a heart for boxing.

The themes behind *Rocky II* should raise questions in the viewer. Why am I here? What is my vocation? Where are my talents and how may I best use them?

A few men know early on what they want to do with their lives. Many more may make wrong decisions or follow ill-planned dreams. Still many, many more men seem to move into a lifetime of toil without giving their purpose in life much thought at all.

Rocky II illustrates the value of knowing our heart's desire, evaluating how well that desire matches our talents and our determination, and then following that desire toward its realization. A few, as I said earlier, discern their destiny in childhood. The rest of us must flail about for a while, as Rocky does in the movie, before we find ourselves striding down the right path.

Bad Boys

In high school, so goes the myth, girls date the star athletes, the actors, the comedians, and the bad boys—the rebels, the guys who drive fast, drink or do drugs, the guys with an edge. Geeks and wonks may score 2400 on their SATs, win medals for the National Latin Exam, or play first violin in the city orchestra, but according to the myth they are losers in the dating game.

There is some truth to this myth. The athletes in high school, the comedians, the good dancers, the wild and the reckless do in fact attract the attention of the opposite sex. Solid reasons account for this phenomenon. For one, high schools are artificial environments, prisons of a sort where certain assumptions drive the behavior of the inmates. The customs of the high school lunch line and the locker room differ radically from the customs of the corporate office and the shop floor. The gifted athlete and the moody rebel attract positive attention for skills and behavior that the workplace would regard as unimportant or even negative qualities. For another, teenage girls, like teenage boys, are attracted by appearances, by the outward rather than the inward, by a young man's height and the cut of his jaw rather than by the fact that he might be a saint in the eyes of her parents or the winner of the National Science Award.

From a male standpoint, and from the standpoint of your own future, the rebels are the most dangerous of these prototypes. If you run with a wild bunch, if you then reach your mid-twenties without killing or maiming yourself, and if you still pride yourself at age twenty-five on your ability to drink whiskey all night and remain on your feet, or on the number of women you can bed and discard, you are likely to discover that women find you much less attractive than you find yourself. You may look like a grownup, you may wear a man's clothes to work and even do a man's job, but you will eventually appear less and less attractive to women, at least to the sort of women you envision as bearing your children and sharing your life. F. Scott Fitzgerald once wrote that "There are no second chances in America," and in this case he was right. A guy who looks at a woman as a piece of meat or who loves Jim Beam as much as he loves Mary Grace is a guy who needs to give up his dream of a good wife and a happy home. He is stuck permanently in adolescence, and most women by this point want men instead of boys.

This is not to say that adult women prefer nerds to adventurers— bankers to buccaneers, so to speak. Despite our modern propaganda, most women want men who are macho, but they want them grown up. They want a man who will protect them without locking them up in a jailhouse of jealousy, a man who can stick to his guns without blowing himself to pieces, a man who can compromise without giving up his soul.

Movies give us many examples of this transition from adult adolescence to adulthood. Director Hugh Wilson's *Blast From The Past* presents us with a man who is the exact opposite of a bad boy but who lacks maturity. Having lived since birth with his parents in a bomb shelter for thirty years—they are convinced that they have survived World War III—Adam (Brendan Fraser) goes out into the world seeking supplies and information. Leaving the shelter, he enters the 1990s as a bright, compassionate innocent who speaks several languages, dances like Fred Astaire, and punches like a good middleweight. Soon he meets Eve (Alicia Silverstone). She has lived a hard life, cheated by various boyfriends and employers, and has grown bitter during her own transition into adulthood. Eve first befriends Adam, and then falls in love with him.

After Eve explodes at Adam for wanting to date a woman she detests, Troy (Dave Foley), Eve's gay friend, has a conversation with Adam during which he explains that Eve doesn't need a boy in her life, but a "man." At that point, Adam, who would qualify as a thirty-something adolescent geek, takes on the mantle of manhood. By becoming stronger himself, he enables Eve to become stronger and more true to herself in her own right.

(Note: In *Blast From the Past, Bridget Jones Diary,* and other movies, the main female character often has a gay male friend. Though this film device may seem a cliché, the reality is that many women do indeed have gay men as their confidants. The attraction here is obvious. A woman can take advice and gain insight into the male mind from a gay friend without the risk of love and pain.)

While *Blast From The Past* depicts a geek growing into manhood, other films show "bad boys" finally taking on the responsibilities of being men. In Nancy Meyers' *Something's Gotta Give,* we meet Harry Sanborn (Jack Nicholson), age sixty-three, a professional bachelor who delights in snagging women half his age. While dating his latest conquest, Marin (Amanda Peet), Harry meets Marin's mother, playwright Erica Barry (Diane Keaton). Erica soon finds herself strongly attracted to Harry, but after a short love affair, she catches Harry once again dating a younger woman.

Heart-broken, Erica eventually has her revenge by writing Harry into a play which makes him a laughingstock on Broadway. Despite these trials, he discovers himself smitten with Erica. His love for a mature woman—Erica is in her mid-fifties—causes Harry to grow from an adolescent to manhood. His wake-up call occurs during an argument after Erica has spotted him in a restaurant with a young model. She runs away, and after chasing her down a sidewalk outside the restaurant, Harry finds himself torn by his desire for Erica and by his habitual practice of pursuing other women. In the following dialogue we see that he truly has remained stuck in his adolescence in his regard for women:

Harry: The truth is, I…I just…don't know how to be a boyfriend.

Erica: That's all you have to say after all of this? That you don't know how to be a boyfriend?

The contempt Erica pushes into that word "boyfriend"—both of them are, after all, well into mid-life—and her abrupt departure crack the walls of the fortress Harry has built around his soul. After suffering what he believes is another heart attack, Harry explores his past with women and realizes how truly ignorant he is about love. In his mid-sixties, having understood at last the pain his infidelities and selfishness have caused, he finally becomes a grown-up.

Many movies, of course, portray the classic adolescent rebel and how he either does—or more frequently, does not—make the transition to manhood. From the 1950s, when Hollywood began pitching movies specifically at teenagers, directors and writers have created such anti-heroes as James Dean in *Rebel Without A Cause*, Dean again in *East of Eden*, and Marlon Brando in *The Wild One*. (When a girl asks Brando, the leader of a motorcycle gang, "What are you rebelling against, Johnny?" he replies: "Whattaya got?")

Coming out of the buttoned-down fifties, these movies created a film genre that has persisted to our own time—the rebellious teenager, usually male, who both longs for, and declines, adulthood. The range of these films is broad, running from the Beach Party movies of the early sixties to today's slasher and horror flicks, from feel-good sports movies to gangsta rap films. With the explosion of the youth culture in the 1960s, and with television eating up much of the adult movie market, Hollywood began marketing more and more to younger audiences, an audience with fewer commitments than adults and with cash to spend at the movies.

Although most of these films are trivial, some of them make important statements on rebellion and maturity. *The Blackboard Jungle, Over the Edge, The Outsiders, A Clockwork Orange, Stand and Deliver*: these and other films offer young men a chance to compare their lives to those of the characters and to discover different escapes from the street and from drugs.

Rumble Fish, for example, delivers a fine meditation on stunted adolescence and on becoming a man. Through most of the movie we watch Rusty James (Matt Dillon) idolizing his older brother, Motorcycle Boy (Mickey Rourke), an aging neighborhood tough guy. The irony here is that Motorcycle Boy knows his limitations, knows that he is a big fish in a tiny pond. He knows, too, that to remain as he is—a boy in a man's body—will spell his ultimate doom, yet he feels powerless to change his ways.

Some movies reveal successful attempts at altering the lives of young men in trouble. Ramon Menendez's *Stand and Deliver* dramatizes the true story of Jaime Escalante (Edward James Olmos) and his teaching of math to young people in East Los Angeles. By teaching the values of discipline and hard work to his impoverished Hispanic students, Escalante lures them away from the culture of drugs and disorder in which they are immersed.

Three male characters—Angel (Lou Phillips), Pancho (Will Gotay), and Tito (Mark Eliot)—represent, respectively, the hard case, the jock, and the lover. The interaction of Escalante with all three is instructive. He shows them love and respect by being tough with them and by making them work up to their potential. By dint of his efforts, these young men realize they can escape a life of poverty and second-hand dreams, that they possess the ability to defeat their harsh circumstances.

In *The Emperor's Club,* set in a private school and worlds away from the hard-knock life of the streets of Los Angeles, another teacher, William Hundert (Kevin Kline), also combines idealism with toughness in dealing with his students. Unlike the Hispanic students of *Stand and Deliver,* the young men in *The Emperor's Club* come from a world of privilege and relative wealth. In his efforts to inspire them to look beyond their material wealth, Hundert gives them examples of men to imitate from the classical world of Greece and Rome.

One day a new student, Sedgewick Bell (Emile Hirsch), the son of a senator, enters Hundert's classroom. A trouble-maker who has been kicked out of several schools and who is at odds with his father, Sedgewick nearly overturns the order of the classroom before Hundert convinces him that he can win academic achievement and take pride in attaining a goal through hard work. But *The Emperor's* Club is not a typical "feel-good" movie; Hundert's mentoring efforts fail, and he catches Sedgewick cheating in the Mr. Caesar contest, a classical quiz bowl attended by Sedgewick's father.

The movie then flashes forward to Sedgewick as an adult and his decision to run for Congress. Seemingly for old-time's sake, he invites his former classmates and teacher to his vast estate for a reunion and a replay of the Mr. Caesar contest. Sedgewick seems to have reformed, but once again Hundert, who is serving as master of ceremonies for the contest, discovers Sedgewick cheating—a graduate student in classics is sending him the answers by an earphone. Hundert then asks a question which the graduate student cannot answer. Once again Sedgewick Bell loses the contest.

Afterwards, the two men confront each other in the restroom. Sedgewick Bell admits his cheating, but sneers at Mr. Hundert's sense of honor.

Mr. Hundert: All of us are at some point forced to look at ourselves in the mirror and see who we really are. When that day comes for you, Sedgewick, you will be confronted with a life lived without virtue, without principle, and for that I pity you. End of lesson.

Sedgewick Bell: What can I say, Mr. Hundert? (a pause) Who gives a shit? (more forcefully) Honestly, who out there gives a shit about your principles? I mean— look at you. What do you have to show for yourself? I live in the real world where people do what they need to do to get what they want. If it's lying and it's cheating, then so be it. I am going to go out there and I am going to win this election and you will see me everywhere. And I'll worry about my contribution later.

Then a toilet flushes. Both men turn, the stall door swings open, and Sedgewick Bell's adolescent son steps out. He stares a moment at his father, his face a mask of pain and disbelief, and leaves the restroom.

Bell doesn't change in the movie. He remains loyal to his own twisted code—winning is all, honor and truth are for losers—and goes on to run for political office. At the end of the film, Hundert regards Bell as a failure, one of his own failures as a teacher, but he also recognizes the scores of other young men on whom he has exerted a positive influence.

The Emperor's Club serves as a warning of what happens to those whose code takes them to the gutter rather than to the stars. In Sedgewick Bell, we see the boy who refused his full manhood, the rebellious adolescent who destroys rather than builds, who works a wrecking ball rather than a hammer and nail. He is as much a hoodlum as any of the other bad boys in film, but with the power and money to do much greater damage.

Transformers

As we have seen in the previous chapter, viewers normally associate coming of age movies with the teenage crowd. Hollywood has produced dozens of these films, movies in which a boy undergoes some traumatic test and emerges from the struggle more mature and on his way to adulthood. Many of the movies reviewed in this book contain such a character.

Of course, not only the young need guidance in growing up. Those adult male adolescents discussed earlier in the book may also require a boost. Here we don't have as many films to pick from. Too often the film industry has created boorish, though often hilarious, images of adult adolescents through movies like *Dumb and Dumber*, *Jackass*, and the Jackie Chan and Luke Wilson series. Nevertheless, Hollywood has made some fine movies about characters giving up their adult adolescence and growing into manhood.

In *Tender Mercies*, Mac Sledge (Robert Duvall) is a broken-down country singer, drunk, flat-out of money, divorced, and abandoned by his agent and friends. In return for pumping gas and performing light repairs at a roadside motel in Texas, Mac receives room and board from Rosa Lee (Tess Harper), a young widow who lost her husband in Vietnam and who now owns the motel, where she is raising her only child, Sonny (Allen Hubbard). Rosa Lee is a Christian (Mac begins going to church with her and later gets baptized), who practices her faith but who also lives with her eyes open.

Though wary of Mac and his drinking, she gives him a job doing maintenance at the motel, and the two of them slowly fall in love. Mac stops his drinking, acts as a friend and adviser to a band of young country singers, becomes a father to Sonny, and marries Rosa Lee. Life continues to batter him—his daughter dies in a car accident, his agent tells him to get lost, his ex-wife curses and scorns him—but Mac now handles adversity with a sober maturity. He wins his battle over the bottle, and so forges on in his new life.

Near the end of the movie, Mac is hoeing in a garden, a dusty patch of land possibly representing Eden and Mac's own bit of paradise. "I never trusted happiness," he says to Rosa Lee. This line, which links him to most adults, male or female, who have lived hard lives, serves as an important capstone for the film. Few real adults trust happiness; they treasure it, they enjoy it, but they know that happiness, unlike joy, is transitory, that the winds of circumstance and caprice can blow contentment away in an instant.

In his book *The Road Less Traveled*, M. Scott Peck began his first chapter with a paragraph of three words: "Life is difficult." Peck then goes on to explain that if we accept this statement, if we acknowledge that life is full of catastrophes minor and major, then paradoxically our own lives become less difficult. By facing life without alcohol and by accepting responsibility for himself and for Rosa Lee and Sonny, Mac has started down Peck's road toward a greater maturity.

Some of you may know men who have spent most of their adult lives as boys. Women are objects to such boy-men, collectibles, notches on a gun belt; intimacy begins and ends with sex. These men love their toys: the latest electronic gadgets, sports cars, the grand vacations. Usually they lack the ties of a wife, children, and a home. Though our culture assumes that these men are to be envied—these are the Playboy men— they strike many observers as lonely, somewhat useless, and even silly.

It is instructive to look again at the film *Something's Gotta Give*. We have examined Harry (Jack Nicholson) and his pride in dating women young enough to be his granddaughters. The movie shows us several other sides of Harry's stunted adulthood: he owns rap music companies, drives a convertible, plays the music of his youth, and is famous enough as a philandering bachelor to be featured in a magazine.

In his relationships with women, Harry is emotionally closer in age to thirty—or even twenty—than he is to sixty-five. Though he himself doesn't recognize his dilemma, his refusal to grow up has damaged him, cutting him off from the deeper joys of intimacy and commitment. Eventually, as stated earlier, he changes, declaring to Erica at the end of the movie: "For the first time in my life I'm in love."

The movie's most important lines, however, are not spoken between Harry and Erica but between Erica and her daughter Marin. Devastated by Harry's desertion, Erica sits weeping on the steps of her beach house when Marin comes outside.

Marin: Oh, mom, I hate this. Now do you get my theory about all this? You gotta self-protect.

Erica: You don't really buy this stuff you say, do you? You don't actually think that you can outsmart getting hurt?

Marin: I think it's worth trying.

Erica: Listen to me. You can't hide from love for the rest of your life because maybe it won't work out...maybe you'll come unglued.

Marin: Are you telling me this is good? What's happened to you?

Erica: I think you should consider that you and I are more alike than you realize. I let someone in, and I had the time of my life.

Marin: I've never had the time of my life.

Erica: I know, baby. And I say this from the deepest part of my heart. What are you waiting for?

This signature moment doesn't belong solely to Erica. Harry, of course, eventually realizes that he too could have the time of his life with Erica, that intimacy beyond a one-night stand offers a treasure of rich delights.

Perhaps the finest movie ever made about a male adolescent adult coming of age is *Groundhog Day*. Here Phil (Bill Murray), an egocentric Pittsburg weatherman who wants more money and power, and who treats his underlings like dirt, drives to Punxsutawney, Pennsylvania, to cover Groundhog Day. After the ceremony, a blizzard shuts down the highways, and Phil, his cameraman Larry (Chris Elliott), and Rita (Andie MacDowell) find themselves stuck overnight in Punxsutawney. Grousing about the storm, Phil goes back to the bed and breakfast where he had stayed the previous night.

Awaking the next morning, Phil finds himself repeating the events of Groundhog Day. He exchanges the same words with the owner of the bed and breakfast; he meets the same people in the streets; the dignitaries once again pull the groundhog from its cage to makes its proclamation about spring. This repetition of days continues: morning after morning, Phil awakens to find himself stuck in the same day.

Locked into this endless cycle of days, this purgatory of the present, Phil at first gives way to his wildest desires, getting his kicks, robbing an armored car, eating every dessert in a restaurant, seducing a woman, repeatedly committing suicide. Yet nothing—not even taking the groundhog hostage—breaks the crazy pattern of time. Phil seems doomed to live out the same day over and over again.

After getting past the despair of reliving his life in this way, of engaging in meaningless binging in food and sex, Phil finally takes advantage of this repetition of days. He changes. He learns to make sculptures from ice, to speak French, to play the piano. He performs good deeds, rescuing some townspeople from physical harm, and becomes a hero to the locals. Most importantly, he comes to know and love Rita. Only when he finally learns to love others, only when he fully reaches his potential—the good part of him, the manly part—does his perpetual Groundhog Day end. He wakes with Rita at his side, free now to enter into life a new man, a whole man.

Groundhog Day makes some important points about becoming a man. First, we come to understand that Phil possesses free will. Eventually, he chooses how he will live his life—in this case, for the good of the community and for his own good. He stops feeling sorry for himself or worrying about getting ahead, and begins noticing the townspeople and their problems. He develops compassion for those around him; he has the leisure to become a part of their lives, to know them, to see how they struggle. After many trials and lessons, he finally develops into a fuller human being. He gets Groundhog Day right.

We also see Phil physically changing into an adult. Here Bill Murray performs brilliantly, giving us in the "grown-up" Phil a man who stands taller, whose voice is steady and modulated, who looks at people rather than past them. He is publicly modest about his many accomplishments. He learns to serve others. He learns that giving truly is more a blessing than receiving. He grows out of himself and into the lives of others.

Phil enters Punxsutawney a whining, cynical, aging adolescent. He departs a man.

Zuzu's Petals

The ability to face up to reality is the Grand Canyon separating men from boys.

The words themselves—"facing up to reality," "looking facts in the face," or similar variations—can slap our dreams like a bucket of ice water. As stated in the last chapter, Scott Peck begins his book *The Road Less Traveled* with a three-word paragraph—"Life is difficult"—and in the next paragraph explains that if human beings accept these words as true, then life itself becomes far less daunting. If put into action, Peck's simple yet brilliant axiom would carry most of us through many a bad time. Rather than be surprised by difficulty, we would expect it.

Yet many of us devise a myriad of ways to avoid the idea that "life is difficult." In addition to alcohol, the traditional defense against the intrusions of the real world, we moderns have other buffers to shield us from pain, duty, and responsibility: drugs, radio, movies, television, books, magazines, computerized pornography, games of all sorts. We take vacations daily from lives our ancestors might have regarded as paradise on earth. To escape reality rather than to accept it, much less change that reality, is the order of the day for many Americans.

Becoming a man means facing up to reality. Though these words may seem grim, Scott Peck is correct in his diagnosis of our condition: acceptance of reality softens its hard edge. To face up to our troubles, to understand that life is difficult, takes away much of the fear and pain we may be feeling. We can then move toward a possible solution to our problems.

The same admonition applies to our ambitions. All men are dreamers, but we must bear in mind that in the real world dreams are never free. They come with a cost. Even dreams unfulfilled, dreams of women, money, power, heroism, come with the psychic cost exacted by the gaping differences between our dreams and the reality of our lives.

Hollywood offers hundreds of examples of men pursuing their dreams while confronting the demands of reality. Sports movies in particular, as we have observed, emotionally sway their audiences by showing what a team or individual must endure to win, to mold reality from dreams. In *Rocky*, for example, we follow the fighter as he trains for his bout with the world champion, doing sit-ups and pushups in dirty gyms, rising before dawn for roadwork, punching cow ribs in a cold-locker freezer.

One sports movie that rises above most of its competitors is *Cinderella Man*. Though the formula for the movie remains basically the same, a hero battling against the odds to become champion, *Cinderella Man* gives us a hero who fights not for glory alone, but also to provide for his wife and children.

When Jim Braddock (Russell Crowe) first appears on screen, he is a fighter at the top of his game, winning money and investing it, living in a suburb in New Jersey with his wife and young children. With the onset of the Depression and a streak of bad luck, we next see Braddock living in a rundown apartment, with the bills piling up and little work to be had in the ring or on the docks. After the electricity to the apartment is cut off in midwinter, and his wife sends the children to live with relatives, Braddock is reduced to going on welfare and even begging money from sportswriters who once covered his big fights.

When his manager offers Braddock a chance to return to the ring, his wife Mae (Renee Zellweger) tells him she doesn't want him to fight anymore. Even after he explains to her why he is fighting—"I have to believe that when things are bad I can change them"—Mae is unhappy with his decision. Later, when Braddock finds himself facing champion Max Baer (Craig Bierko), a fierce opponent who has already killed two men in the ring, Mae redoubles her efforts to convince him to stop boxing. Just before the fight, Mae finally catches a glimpse of why her husband is going into the ring against Baer and throws her support into his corner with these words:

Mae: Maybe I understand, some, about having to fight. So you just remember who you are…You're the Bulldog of Bergen, and the Pride of New Jersey, you're everybody's hope, and the kids' hero, and you are the champion of my heart, James J. Braddock."

What man wouldn't fight like a champion with such a woman backing him?

Like other inspirational sports movies, *Cinderella Man* ends with Braddock as champion not only of the world but also of his impoverished family. (Asked by the press what he is fighting for, Braddock replies, "Milk.") What makes this movie important and rare among such films is its examination of Braddock's love for his family and the effects of poverty and debt on that family. Any man who has ever gone deeply into debt, or faced eviction, any man who has suffered the diminished sense of self brought about by debt and poverty, will feel the pain of the family in these scenes.

Fewer in number, but perhaps more important to the ordinary man lacking athletic ability or inclination, are those movies in which the hero battles adversaries not found on a basketball court or inside a boxing ring. *The Pursuit of Happyness* (this misspelling is intentional and derives from a scene in the movie) depicts the ordeal of Chris Gardner (Will Smith). Poor, abandoned by his wife, and responsible for the care of his young son, Gardner tries to escape his poverty and give his son a home by entering a training program at a prestigious Wall Street brokerage firm. Gardner recognizes the challenges he faces: the lost hours of sleep, the nerve-racking schedule of deadlines in the brokerage, the daily task of caring for his son while working and studying. But it is this recognition and acceptance of reality—"life is difficult"—that allows him to move forward toward the realization of his dreams. As he tells his son, Christopher (Jaden Smith): "You got a dream…you gotta protect it. People can't do something for themselves, they wanna tell you you can't do it. If you want something, go get it. Period."

Here Gardner casts a gimlet eye on the nay-sayers around him. Like an athlete who won't let others psych him out, Gardner ignores the dire words of those who would pull him down.

For those who have faced reality in this way, *The Pursuit of Happyness,* like *Cinderella Man*, is a painful movie to watch, a pointed reminder that the realities of life can be pricked, barbed, and bladed with pain, and that this pain may only be beaten by first acknowledging it.

Master and Commander, a film about naval warfare during the Napoleonic wars and perhaps the best all-round movie in this book about the tests of manhood, features Captain Jack Aubrey (Russell Crowe). Here is a man who never blinks in the face of facts, no matter how insurmountable they may appear. He encourages others to do the same. He understands that the inability to face up to those facts may result in turmoil, death, the sinking of his ship. When he sees a sailor deliberately show disrespect to one of his midshipmen, he has the sailor clapped in irons and upbraids the midshipman for allowing the incident to occur in the first place. When another young midshipman, no more than a boy, loses an arm during combat, Aubrey makes him a gift of a biography of Lord Nelson, England's finest captain of that era, in which there is a picture of Nelson missing one of his own arms. In his pursuit of his French rival, Aubrey hopes for the best—the defeat and capture of that ship—but recognizes the obstacles standing in his way. He is a realist, a true leader who knows the pain and cost of achieving his dreams.

And sometimes, of course, we fail. We don't always get what we want. Despite Chris Gardener's advice to his son to "go get it," sometimes "it" simply can't be gotten. Our failure to achieve our dreams may derive from our own inadequacy, our inability to measure up to the magnitude of the dream, a failure of the will, or circumstances beyond our control. We may beat our fists against the walls, we may roar like wounded beasts, we may curse or pray until curses and prayers become one, but sometimes nothing changes. Despite all our planning and good intentions, our dreams go down the tubes, and we either adjust or spend the rest of our lives soured by bitterness and regret.

Here movies are less help as mentors. In some sense, movies, like so many stories, tell fairy tales. Directors and writers tell us little about failure—not because they don't understand it, but because a story of failure is a harder sell at the box office. No one, for example, wants to watch a war movie that ends with the hero dead and his cause lost.

Yet one movie does offer us an instructive look at what can happen to a man who fails to attain his dreams. Frank Capra's classic, *It's A Wonderful Life*, tells the story of George Bailey (Jimmy Stewart), who has big dreams of travel and college. We follow George from his youth, when as a soda jerk he vows to explore the world, to his young adulthood, when he seems on the verge of achieving his visions of adventure in the wide world outside of Bedford Falls. Here he tells Mary (Donna Reed), who will someday be his wife, what he wants:

"I'm shaking the dust of this crummy town off my feet and I'm gonna see the world. Italy, Greece, the Parthenon, the Colosseum. Then, I'm comin' back here to go to college and see what they know. And then I'm gonna build things. I'm gonna build airfields, I'm gonna build skyscrapers a hundred stories high, I'm gonna build bridges a mile long...."

But there will be no skyscrapers or bridges for George. Reality claws at his dreams, forcing him to support his younger brother at college, to take over the family business, a building and loan association, to fight against the schemes of a wicked businessman seeking to run the town, to sacrifice his own ambitions in order to help others in Bedford Falls achieve theirs. Whatever qualms he has about his choices, George again and again foregoes his dreams and lays himself on the altar of sacrifice for his friends.

Such sacrifices run counter to our culture today. Chris Gardener's "If you want something, go get it" seems in some ways deeply opposed to George Bailey's choices in *It's A Wonderful Life*. To understand a little of why George Bailey made his decisions, we must look to the scene where George, still grieving his father's death, faces Mr. Potter, the greedy villain of the film who hopes to take over the Bailey Building and Loan:

"Now hold on, Mr. Potter. You're right when you say my father was no business-man. I know that. Why he ever started this cheap, penny-ante Building and Loan, I'll never know. But neither you nor anyone else can say anything against his character...Just remember this, Mr. Potter, that this rabble you're talking about—they do most of the working and paying and living and dying in this community. Well, is it too much to have them work and pay and live and die in a couple of decent rooms and a bath? Anyway, my father didn't think so. People were human beings to him. But to you, a warped, frustrated old man, they're cattle. Well, in my book he died a much richer man than you'll ever be."

For George, character and obligation override ambition. When his dreams crash into reality, it is the dreams that must yield. He gives up his plans for travel to run his father's business; he gives up his opportunity for higher education so that his brother may advance himself; he gives up his honeymoon to save his business and the town in which he lives.

When on Christmas Eve George's Uncle Billy loses a large bank deposit belonging to the building and loan—the money is actually stolen by Mr. Potter—George finally suffers the breakdown that has been so long in coming. He crawls to Mr. Potter for help, wounds his family with shouted insults, and goes to a bridge over the town's river intending to commit suicide. (In one of the more touching scenes in motion picture history, his wife Mary understands that something has gone wrong and doesn't condemn George for his insults and shouts. Instead, she tells her children to pray for their father and calls the town together to help him.)

At the bridge, George is rescued by his guardian angel Clarence Oddbody (Henry Travers). Clarence then gives George a chance to look at his past as if George hadn't existed, as if he had never been born. Both George and the audience see how diminished and tragic the world would have been without him. Because George saved his brother's life in their childhood, his brother, a fighter pilot, saved the lives of hundreds of sailors in World War II. Because of George's many sacrifices, he helped create rich, full lives for his mother, his wife, and his children. Because of his battles against Potter, he kept Bedford Falls from a future of poverty and decay.

"Why was I born?" "What's the point to my life?" "What good have I ever done?" Such questions may bombard us, as they do George Bailey, when the world has taken a flamethrower to our aspirations and dreams. And like George, we too may stand at the brink of an abyss, ready to be swallowed up by despair and hopelessness.

It's A Wonderful Life gives us a way to turn our backs on that abyss. Instead of asking "Why was I born?" the movie asks "What if I had never been born?" and "What does my life mean to others?" These questions point us outward, away from the confines of our own hearts, and allow us to see the good we have brought to others.

Navigating this tension between what we ask from life and what life gives us makes us better men.

Part III
Men and Women

"What do women want?"

—Sigmund Freud

Treat Her Like A Lady

Sigmund Freud's famous question—"What do women want?"—crosses the lips of most men at one time or another. Goaded by desire, love, frustration, or failure, we open our investigation, searching for clues to the conundrums of womanhood, some fingerprint, some bit of DNA, that will unveil the mysteries of the female heart and mind. Often, however, our sleuthing leads only to greater confusion. Like Churchill's Russia, the female of the species remains for us "a riddle wrapped in a mystery inside an enigma."

One difficulty with Freud's question, of course, lies with the question itself. Its imprecision guarantees confusion; its breadth makes reckoning the origins of the universe a simple task by comparison. Women are individuals, and men attempting to reduce their nature to a universal formula run into trouble.

If we refine the question, however, we find the possibility of an answer. Lately, for instance, I have fashioned this related question: What do most women want in men in the initial stages of a relationship? Is it possible to isolate one element that first attracts women to men? How, for instance, would a single man like myself—I'm a widower, sixty some years old, stocky in build, with one child still in college and a minimum of savings—win the affections of a female?

Having squandered a good amount of time pondering this question, having dated several different women with varying success, and having read female comments on various online dating services, I believe I possess the answer:

Women want a gentleman.

It's true that in polls and on internet dating services women say they are looking for other qualities in a man. Many women claim to desire in men what society once deemed feminine merits: sensitivity, the ability to listen, empathy. Others cite power and money, and surprisingly, humor, as desirable traits in men. Fewer seem to require handsome men, though most women doubtless prefer a partner who can chew pizza with his mouth closed and who weighs less than a grand piano.

From what I have observed and experienced, however, what a woman wants most from a first date is a gentleman. She wants a man with manners and a sense of civility, a man who respects her, who puts her on a bit of a pedestal—not too grand a pedestal, but a pedestal nonetheless. (To use an example from *Gone With The Wind*, women want Ashley Wilkes for his manners and ideals, but enjoy a little of "Bad Boy" Rhett Butler thrown into the equation as well.) A woman wants a man who can write a love letter or sit comfortably through the opening night of *Sex and the City*, but who can also change a flat tire, work the yard, and defend her against assailants.

She wants, in short, a man who is both gentle and manly.

We should not be surprised that women prefer gentlemen. It was, after all, a woman, Eleanor of Aquitaine, a fiery feminist for her day, who long ago helped devise the idea of a gentleman-knight and the values of courtly love. Singing ballads and composing poems about knights, damsels in distress, and rescued maidens, troubadours planted Eleanor's vision of noble warriors and virtuous ladies all over Europe during the High Middles Ages. This music and literature grew in influence, and seizing hold of the medieval imagination, caused an upheaval in the way men treated women. Women became more than just property, bearers of heirs, managers of households; they were, in the eyes of men, fellow creatures worthy of noble deeds, passion, and love. This code of chivalry and manners in regard to women endured some thirty-five generations, becoming ever more refined in response to changing times. Even the pioneers of our own raw frontier practiced this code, as may be seen in the chronicles of our Wild West, where a woman who played the lady could cross the continent unharmed and esteemed among rough, violent men.

In the second half of the twentieth century, this code of etiquette came under attack. Radical assaults on the foundations of Western Civilization shook the pillars of sexual civility and decorum. In the consequent wreckage, men found themselves lost without maps, survivors of an earthquake who could no longer recognize a landscape once their own. In certain circles, to call a woman a lady was forbidden, to open a door for a woman was to risk verbal abuse, to offer a seat on a public conveyance to a woman was to invite the label of misogynist. Stare at a woman at work, or offer some offhand comment about her appearance, and you could find yourself standing in an unemployment line. Many college campuses set up sexual conduct codes, reducing the calculus of love and romance to a sort of joyless elementary school arithmetic.

The first decade of the new millennium has seen the emergence of a wistful longing for the old code of manners. Many commentators honored the manly courage of the firefighters, police, and soldiers who died in the 9/11 attacks. Some areas of the country have seen a renewed interest in etiquette classes for adolescents, and the media reports that even native New Yorkers have softened their rough edges in the last few years. A good number of young women still dream, surreptitiously and discretely, of the knight on the white horse, only now they want him modernized. They want men who will treat them like ladies, but without condescension. They desire decorum and courtesy, but with full recognition of their talents and their rights to equality in education and employment.

Unfortunately, the passage of courteous conduct from one generation to the next requires teachers or exemplars, and the assaults of the last fifty years have thinned the ranks of both ladies and gentlemen. With mentors in short supply, chivalry and its mistress, romance, sometimes seem moribund. We sneer at the Victorians for burying sex beneath crinoline and bowdlerized language, yet what would they make of us, with our crass appetites, our lack of refinement, our taste for violence and crude perversions? Sexual innuendo permeates our advertising. Pornography, formerly confined to adult bookstores in large cities, is now as available online as the weather or the daily news. Among some teenagers "hooking up" has taken the place of dating, grind-dancing the place of their parents' disco. Some parents dress their adolescent girls like whores, then profess shock when some men see them that way. Though many people yearn for a set of rules in the game of love and courtship—a recent book on this subject popular among women was titled *The Rules*—these aspirants to romance lack the living guides who by lesson and example once taught the arts of civility to young women and men.

Despite this deficit of mentors, there is one resource, often overlooked, which does teach men how to behave like gentleman and why this appeals to the ladies. Although much maligned for its contributions to violence and vacuous sex in our society, this low-priced teaching tool nevertheless affords the world's best classroom for the aspiring gentleman.

I am speaking, of course, of Hollywood.

Factory of dreams, fabricator of customs and style, Hollywood has frequently served up portraits of gentlemen and why they attract women. Every man who takes an inventory of his favorite films will surely find one or two in which a knight-errant, modern or medieval, is at the heart of the story. The reviews in this chapter of *Movies Make The Man* provide only a brief introduction to the Hollywood school of manners, class, and conduct.

First up on our short list is Humphrey Bogart as Rick Blaine in *Casablanca*. Here we see the powerful impact of love on the heart and behavior of a man. When we meet Rick, the former idealist has become a hardened cynic who mistreats women and who blithely declares: "I stick my neck out for nobody." Yet when Ilsa, the love of his life, arrives at Rick's cafe, Rick's cynicism gradually gives way to his former idealism. He helps a young Hungarian couple find the money to buy their way to America. He allows the club band to play the "Marseilles," fully aware that the German soldiers drinking and singing in his club may punish him. Finally, he lies to Ilsa's husband Victor Laszlo about his affection for Ilsa, knowing that with his lie he will lose the woman he loves most in the world. Each of these actions reveals the emerging gentleman within Rick Blaine, the "gentle man" who puts the weak and defenseless ahead of his own desires.

Unlike Rick Blaine, *Braveheart*'s William Wallace (Mel Gibson) never gives way to cynicism in the face of hardship, but remains instead an idealist who always acts as a gentleman toward the ladies. Wallace meets his future wife when both are still children. At the funeral for Wallace's father and brother, who have died defending Scotland from the English, a little girl, Murron, gives the orphaned Wallace a stalk of heather. His uncle then takes Wallace away from his home and educates him. He travels to distant places like Rome, learns to speak and read Latin and French, practices the social graces, and becomes acquainted with the arts of war.

But he never forgets his father's farm or Murron. He returns to Scotland to restore the house in which he grew up and to seek out Murron. In one of Hollywood's most romantic scenes, Wallace returns to Murron the heather he has preserved all these years. He courts her, and they are soon married.

Much later, after the murder of his wife, Wallace makes love to the future queen of England. Though this event is fiction, the glaring contrast between Wallace and the weak-chinned, cowardly Edward II reflects the difference between a gentleman and a medieval version of today's metrosexual. The princess desires Wallace not only because he is a fierce warrior with a natural sense of his own masculinity, but also because he treats her like a lady rather than an object.

Whit Stillman's *The Last Days of Disco* is an underrated film offering a much more subtle portrait of a modern gentleman. Though nearly all of the characters, male and female, are shallow and immature, more interested in themselves and their own welfare than in others, two characters do pay homage to a chivalric code greater than themselves. Alice (Chloe Sevigny), a young editorial assistant, undergoes a moral transformation largely through suffering the betrayals and lies of her friends. Alice eventually falls in love with an attorney, Josh Neff (Matt Keeslar). Having suffered an emotional breakdown in college, followed by a religious conversion, Josh acts responsibly toward his position in the district attorney's office (he resigns his coveted post, citing a conflict of interest), toward his friends (he warns them of the coming drug bust at the disco), and toward Alice (whom he clearly loves). Only Josh and Alice show consideration for anyone other than themselves, which is, of course, one of the quintessential marks of etiquette.

Perhaps Hollywood's best study of a gentleman is found in James Mangold's *Kate and Leopold,* a romantic comedy which most women adore, but which few men of my acquaintance have seen. Here Meg Ryan plays Kate, a modern woman looking for corporate success whose personal relationships are failures. Her opposite is Hugh Jackman's Leopold, an English aristocrat from the year 1876, who has inadvertently traveled through time to present-day Manhattan.

When Kate's brother Charlie (Breckin Meyer), an unemployed actor and comedian, befriends and then invites Leopold to supper at Kate's apartment, we receive our first of several lessons contrasting the manners of the nineteenth century with those of modern America. Leopold arrives for supper formally dressed and sits erect while eating; Kate wears scruffy sweats and slouches over her food like a bored teenager. Leopold stands whenever Kate goes to the kitchen— "I am accustomed to rise whenever a lady leaves the table"—a gesture which startles Kate and amuses Charlie. The supper served up by Kate—an overcooked piece of unidentifiable meat, tater tots, and a mediocre salad—Leopold finds inedible, declaring his own society believes that "without the culinary arts, the crudeness of reality would be unbearable."

Though we see Leopold make an impression on Kate in several subsequent scenes—Leopold, for example, gallantly recovers Kate's briefcase from a mugger—his gentlemanly conduct and its effect on women may best be seen on the night Kate goes to supper with her boss, J.J. (Bradley Whitford). At the same time, Charlie takes Leopold to a club to meet Patrice (Charlotte Ayanna), a young woman to whom Charlie is attracted. After Leopold becomes the center of attention when he mentions having explored the basement of the Louvre—Patrice was an art major at Vassar—Charlie takes him to task for dominating Patrice's affections:

Charlie: Patrice—she thought you were cute. Probably gay and cute. And cute, Leo, is the kiss of death.

Leopold: Perhaps. But I believe this is her number (He hands Charlie a napkin with the telephone number written on it). As I see it, Patrice has not an inkling of your affections. And it's no wonder. You, Charles, are a Merry Andrew.

Charlie: A what?

Leopold: Everything plays a farce for you. Women respond to sincerity. This requires pulling one's tongue from one's cheek. No one wants to be romanced by a buffoon (nods at the napkin). Now that number rings her.

Charlie: Yeah?

Leopold: So ring her tomorrow.

Charlie: I can't. She gave the number to you.

Leopold: Only because I told her of your affections.

Charlie (stopping suddenly): Wh—what did you say?

Leopold: Merely that you admired her but that you were hesitant to make an overture since you'd been told she was courting another.

Charlie: Shit—that's good. What did she say?

Leopold: She handed me the napkin.

In the next scene, director Mangold offers us another glaring contrast, this time between Leopold and J.J., a man of pretension and false sophistication. On the way home from their evening with Patrice, Charlie and Leopold swing by the restaurant where J.J. and Kate are dining. When J.J. claims to speak French, to own an old English manor house, and to love opera, Leopold exposes him as a poseur, and then tells J.J., who is clearly pursuing Kate, that "some feel that to court a woman in one's employ is nothing more than a serpentine effort to transform a lady into a whore."

Other scenes confirm Leopold's status as a quintessential gentleman. He writes what Kate's secretary calls the "best apology letter in the history of mankind." He scripts the telephone call Charlie makes to Patrice, helping Charlie to secure his long-standing desire to date her. He behaves impeccably in treating Kate like a lady.

We can't all be Hugh Jackman, who is, quite literally, "tall, dark, and handsome." Nor can we revert to the formal language and manners of the nineteenth century. With some help from Hollywood, however, we can learn something about being gentlemen. In the practice of etiquette, most of us need a few repairs rather than a major renovation, and the cinema gives us hints on making these changes. What is required from us is thought and interest. After all, learning how to attract the women we wish to pursue is really not that difficult.

In the words of Leopold to Charlie, "Think of pleasing her, not vexing her."

Close Encounters of the First Kind

You're on a first date. It's your first real encounter with the young woman, and you want to make a good impression. You've introduced yourselves, taken a table in the restaurant, and sit opposite one another. The candle on the table glitters, the waiter offers impeccable service, the music in the background is enchanting. The entire universe seems poised for your success.

And then you open your mouth.

Here is where you make it or break it. Women, as we have noted, value speech and the communication of feelings. Your date will be listening to you, antenna on the alert.

So you open your mouth and speak. And what comes out? Do you spend the next hour telling her about your college, your work, your boss, your last relationship or your failed marriage? Do you ramble on for entire paragraphs telling her all your health problems or how much you dislike certain politicians, what music you enjoy or what books you've read? Do you kill your chance for a relationship by giving a blow-by-blow, scene-by-scene analysis of Van Kilmer's latest action flick?

Gentlemen, this first date is not about you. This date is like a waltz—the woman is the picture, the center of attention, and you are the frame. This is the time when she should stand out and you should fade into the background. This is the time, in other words, to listen to her. She'll want to know about you, and you should give her some details, some insights into who you are and what you like, but if you dominate the conversation, the odds are that she will rightly consider you a jerk and look elsewhere for companionship. By making her center-stage, by revealing less of yourself, you'll also arouse her curiosity. You will appear mysterious, and she will be intrigued.

This is the time for you to find out about her. This is your opportunity to discover her preferences in restaurants, foods, and entertainment, so that the next time you go out together you can plan a date aimed at her. Ask plenty of questions. If her ideal of a great Sunday afternoon is a book and a cup of cocoa beside a warm fire, ask her what she likes to read. If she mentions that she likes hiking, ask her where she has hiked. Whether you like reading or hiking at this point is irrelevant. This conversation is not about you. She's the picture; you're the frame.

In addition to asking her questions, this is the time to treat this lady like a queen. No matter how she looks, no matter how she behaves, this is the time when you stand at her arrival at the table; you allow her to order first; you ask if she is enjoying her meal; you put a napkin in your lap; you try to get the food from your plate to your mouth without looking like a steam-shovel. If you haven't worked out payment of the meal before your date, you should firmly offer to pay the bill.

Kate And Leopold, which we previously discussed, provides a glaring contrast in dating and dining. In the first instance, we see J. J., Kate's boss, in a fancy restaurant with Kate. He has lured her there to discuss her possible promotion, but as Kate eventually points out, they have spent the evening discussing everything but her job. Instead, J.J. holds forth on his castle in England (which is not really a castle), his knowledge of opera (which is minimal), and his expertise in food and wine (which is a mark of his pretentiousness). J.J. is a crashing bore, an egotist of the first degree, a deceiver using his position in the company to try and get Kate to sleep with him.

In contrast, when Leopold asks Kate for a date, he plans every detail of their evening together. With candles and flowers, he transforms a city rooftop into a place of intimate romance. He hires a violinist to provide music. He sets up a lovely table and service, and offers Kate an exquisite meal. He says little of himself, but instead aims the entire evening at her.

Even in a movie like *Something's Gotta Give*, the crude millionaire Harry Sanborn woos playwright Erica Barry by focusing his attention on her. When he stays with Erica to recover from his heart attack, the two of them meet in the kitchen for a late night snack of waffles. Here the director shows us why Harry, who up to this point seems only a playboy, is a hit with so many women. His charm and gentle finesse take him past the awkward and embarrassing moments he has experienced with Erica the previous two days. He treats Erica with tenderness and respect, and shows an interest in her life.

In *Henry V*, Kenneth Branagh's fine interpretation of Shakespeare's play, we are again given this lesson. Henry (Kenneth Branagh) has conquered France and now finds himself alone for the first time with the French princess, Katherine (Emma Thompson). She speaks little English, and his own French, as the king acknowledges, is poor. Henry could have acted the part of arrogant conqueror, claiming the affections of the princess as his right. Instead, Shakespeare has Henry express his desire to conquer her heart by romance rather than by force. He deprecates his own achievements, reassures the princess he will treat her with honor, and then begs her to consider him as her suitor with these famous words:

Henry: Yet I love thee too. And while thou liv'st, dear Kate, take a fellow of plain and uncoined constancy, for he perforce must do thee right because he hath not the gift to woo in other places. For these fellows of infinite tongue, that can rhyme themselves into ladies' favors, they do always reason themselves out again. What? A speaker is but a prater, a rhyme is but a ballad, a good leg will fall, a straight back will stoop, a black beard will turn white, a curled pate will grow bald, a fair face will wither, a full eye will wax hollow, but a good heart, Kate, is the sun and the moon, or rather the sun and not the moon, for it shines bright and never changes but keeps his course truly. If thou would have such a one, take me. And take me, take a soldier. Take a soldier, take a king. And what say'st thou then to my love? Speak, my fair, and fairly, I pray thee.

Henry may throw about too many words here, but the gist of his message reveals a plain-speaking fellow with a steadfast heart.

Of course, dating in the real world differs greatly from a Hollywood movie. We don't have a scripted dialogue; no music plays in the background; few of us are as sophisticated as Cary Grant (Even Cary Grant was once quoted as saying that he wished he could be Cary Grant.) Nor, really, should we try to be Cary Grant. The imitation would fit most of us as poorly as a badly hung tuxedo. What we can do, however, is to sit in Hollywood's classroom and take away a few lessons for our own lives.

Whether we are seventeen or seventy-seven, the goals for a first date change very little. The name of the game is to break the ice, begin a conversation, and avoid making fools of ourselves.

Chick Flicks:
What We Can Learn

For many men, women are like Livingstone's Africa: lovely to look upon, uncharted, mysterious, and possibly deadly. To many women, men are obtuse creatures designed by nature with multiple defects: an inability to hear everything said to them, a lack of basic communication skills, a marked deficiency in empathy, a blindness to the power of a kiss, a rose, or a few well-put words.

Movies provide men with a rough map by which they might begin their exploration of women. One crucial part of that map, a part often overlooked by men, consists of movies appealing to women, otherwise known as chick flicks. These are movies men either refuse outright or else attend grudgingly, where they slouch beside their dates, half-defiant and at the same time half-afraid some friend may see them there.

A woman I was dating once asked me to attend the opening night of *Sex and the City*. She was a fan of the hit television series while I, on the other hand, had never watched the show, had no idea of the characters or plot, and didn't realize until entering the theater that the television series and the movie were considered top of the line chick flick material. (My first indication was the audience, which was about ten to one, women to men.)

What I learned in the next two hours about women was worth a hundred times the amount of the admissions ticket, with the lessons coming not from the movie but from the audience. When one of the film's stars received a proposal, the women wildly cheered; when she tried on a wedding dress, the audience literally ooohed and ahhhed. When another character, a hardened and bitter lawyer, castigated her husband for sleeping with another woman—the wife was in some respects responsible for the husband's philandering—the audience booed, with the woman behind me saying several times in a loud whisper: "You bitch! You bitch!" When the heroine of *Sex and the City* realized she had driven her fiancé away and wanted him back, the women cheered and burst into applause.

This was the evening I realized a lynch mob made up of women might be more dangerous than one composed of men.

Sex and the City taught me I could learn much about women from watching such a movie. We don't need to see chick flicks to get in touch with our feminine side (one of the sillier sayings of the sexual revolution). If we seek admission into the minds of women, however, at least on a beginner's level, chick flicks are an excellent way to acquire a few painless lessons. Here two movies, both with female directors, can contribute to our education.

In Nancy Meyers' *What Women Want*, Mel Gibson as Nick Marshall plays an advertising firm executive who is passed over for promotion in favor of a woman, Darcy Maguire (Helen Hunt). That night in his penthouse, half-drunk and experimenting with some beauty products to be advertised by the firm, Nick is struck by lightning and receives the extraordinary gift—and curse—of being able to hear the thoughts of women around him. We follow Nick through the next few days, during which the women he encounters—his exchanges with Lola (Marisa Tomei), a coffee shop cashier, are particularly humorous—share with him by telepathy their fears and desires. Initially, a terrified Nick wants the voices out of his head, but a female psychiatrist finally convinces him his amazing gift will bring him love and power.

Nick uses his newfound gift at a company meeting, reading the minds of the women gathered around him and bringing their silent arguments to the table as if they were his own. (Lola, with whom he has a brief fling, becomes convinced that Nick is gay because he understands women so well.) Eventually, of course, Nick's insights bring him to a new empathy with women, particularly with the women he loves—his daughter and his new boss. By being forced into the thoughts of females whom he had previously exploited or ignored, Nick gains an appreciation for women, with his cavalier lust deepening into love for Darcy.

What Women Want—the title comes, of course, from Freud's famous question—reminds men that what women want from men differs from what men want from women, at least in the initial stages of affection and courtship. In the movie, Nick realizes that women want respect, recognition of their talents, and above all, love. Sex is important to these women—we see sexual passion recognized throughout Nick's mental encounters with women—but they also value affirmation. Lola, Darcy, Nick's daughter, and the female office workers: all seek recognition as persons in their own right. This sense of personhood, this idea that we are individuals unique in our talents and desires, is at the heart of the movie. Nick, who previously had regarded women as objects rather than as individuals worthy of respect, becomes aware of his shortcomings and undergoes a transformation that broadens his views of the opposite sex.

Another helpful film is Sharon Maguire's *Bridget Jones's Diary*. Based on the best-selling novel by Helen Fielding, who also wrote the screenplay, *Bridget Jones's Diary* focuses on a single woman living in London. Bridget Jones is thirty-two year old and wants to find a man who will love her and will commit to a relationship. The first half of the movie brings lots of laughs as Bridget (Renee Zellweger) enters into one embarrassing situation after another, while the second half shows her working out the fact that steadiness and honesty are better valued in a man than glamour and glitter.

At the beginning of the film, Bridget, coming off a drunken New Year's Eve, ponders her loneliness and doesn't like what she sees of her future: "I'd live a life where my major relationship was with a bottle of wine, and I'd finally die fat and alone, and be found three weeks later, half-eaten by wild dogs."

Bridget vows to keep a diary, to tell the truth, as she says, about herself, and in the process to look for the man who will love her. Her diary, with its daily listing of cigarettes smoked, pounds gained and lost, and wine consumed, becomes a barometer of her love life. Here, for example, in a voice-over in the film, Bridget makes her New Year's resolution:

Bridget: Resolution #1: uggg—will obviously lose 20 pounds. #2: always put last night's panties into laundry basket. Equally important: will find new sensible boyfriend and stop forming romantic attachments to any of the following: alcoholics, workoholics, sexoholics, commitment phobics, peeping toms, meglomaniacs, emotional fuckwads, or perverts.

Bridget immediately forgets her resolution when her boss, Daniel Cleaver (Hugh Grant), begins flirting with her. Soon they are sleeping together, but Daniel, who fits about half of the proscribed boyfriends in Bridget's list, quickly lets us and then Bridget see that he is merely using her.

Meanwhile, the high-powered attorney who does fit Bridget's criteria for an ideal boyfriend, Mark Darcy (Colin Firth), has fallen in love with her. Thinking that Bridget is attracted to Daniel, he makes plans to take a job in the United States. After seeing that Daniel is a liar and womanizer, Bridget realizes she actually loves Mark and rushes off to meet him.

For men, *Bridget Jones's Diary* offers some particularly valuable insights into the ways of women. After her disastrous affair with Daniel, for example, we observe Bridget throwing away books with titles like *What Men Want* and *What Men Think*, and replacing them with *How to Get What You Want* and *Women Who Love Men Are Mad.* In another scene, Bridget and three friends, one of them a gay male, intricately plot out what she should do on her first date with Daniel: what she should wear, how she should mingle with the other guests at the party, what to say and not to say.

Here we learn that women read about relationships and approach dating like military strategists, whereas most men simply bumble into romance.

Bridget offers other insights on dating men. We come to understand that she broods on her failed loves, just as men do. We also see how important praise and compliments are to her. She cherishes, for example, Mark Darcy's comment to her "I like you just as you are." Finally, Renee Zellweger as Bridget gives us a realistic woman: she is overweight, sometimes clumsy, makes inappropriate remarks, and falls back on her vices—drinking, smoking, overeating—when struck by love's hard blows.

And here we have the most important lesson of the movie—and perhaps of relationships in general. Despite the makeup, the carefully chosen dresses and shoes, the books about relationships and dating, most women, like most men, are looking for someone who will like them and love them just the way they are.

Sense and Sensitivity

Many women accuse men of being insensitive. Scores of articles and books appear annually describing and analyzing this perception. Men, we are told, are blind and deaf to female wants and needs. We are pig-headed, sloppy, and slothful, stupid about money, addicted to sports and games, prone to violence, inattentive in romance, inept at sex. These stereotypes have become so ingrained in our culture that their implied prejudice often goes unremarked. In fact, like male chauvinists of old, a good number of women not only buy into their own propaganda regarding the faults of men, but also feel free to air these attacks in public, safe in the knowledge, given today's female-sympathetic culture, that most men won't return their shots.

And they're right. Many men harbor resentments regarding such remarks, but we rarely fire back, at least not in female company. We endure these taunts and insults without blinking for different reasons. For one, we understand that society these days cares less about men than women. In my church, for example, we recently prayed "for victims of violence, particularly women and children." What about men? For another, bickering of this sort simply isn't up our alley. It's not in our nature as men. Parents and teachers taught us at a young age "not to hit girls," and most of us took this adage to mean verbally as well as physically. And of course, many of us are unintentionally insensitive. Unlike women, we lack the antennae to pick up the small signals. A friend of mine was recently washing the dishes when a woman he was dating called him. They discussed a matter important to her before they hung up. Later she wrote him an email telling him she felt he wasn't paying attention to her by continuing to scrub the dishes. My friend always moves when on the phone, pacing, tidying up, washing dishes. To sit down to talk on the phone simply never occurred to him.

Some women are sensitive too because they either feel oppressed by men or suffer from a history of oppression. Such feelings strike some modern men as outlandish. Women are in the majority in this country. They live longer lives than men. More women go to college than men and now earn more doctorates than men. They earn salaries equal to men for the same work. Advertisements and television shows generally portray women in a more positive light than men. How, we want to ask, are women oppressed?

Men, on the other hand, can never regard themselves as oppressed by women. It's not a part of the male code. For a man to feel "oppressed" by women is, as the Victorians might say, "simply not done."

This politicization of sex and romance can poison relations between men and women. Take the word "love," for example. Many adults, male and female, particularly those over thirty, tiptoe around the word, fearing what some of them call "the L word" as much as their grandparents once feared communism. The gender politics in the office, at school, and in the public arena, and the obsession of our society with sex, have cast poor love shivering into the cold.

Another reason why men don't argue with women about feelings is that we nearly always lose. Men may win a debate with women about more objective subjects—the chances of the Cubs making the World Series, charcoal versus gas grills, the reasons behind a business downturn—but a man doesn't have a prayer when it comes to arguing with a woman about feelings.

But though we men will continue to lose these arguments, movies can show us, at least to a small extent, how women think about love and romance, and why men sometimes come across as clueless knuckleheads. Watch these movies, and others recommended by the women in your life, and they may add to your understanding of women.

First up on our agenda is *Pride and Prejudice*. Both the book and the movies made about this classic story have the same effect on women that Hemingway's *For Whom The Bell Tolls* exerted on several generations of men. All sorts of spin-offs from Jane Austen's novel exist, but the one you'll want to see—all right, I'll rephrase that, the one you need to see—is the five-hour A&E miniseries starring Jennifer Ehle as Elizabeth Bennet and Colin Firth as Mr. Darcy. Austen's famous quote—"It is a truth universally acknowledged, that a single man in possession of a good fortune, must be in want of a wife"—sums up the movie as well as any long-winded review. Though set in nineteenth century England, *Pride and Prejudice* still serves today as a manual on relationships, marriage, and the maneuverings of men and women in their wars of the heart. That so many young women treasure this story indicates that the yearning for romance in our post-modern world remains alive.

Likely, women also love *Pride and Prejudice* for the beauty of its language. Though some of this language is concocted from literature, Jane Austen and her contemporaries regarded speaking and oration as important life-skills. These people would have regarded as appalling the stumbles and mumbles that pass for conversation today. Listen, for example, to the repartee between several members of *Pride and Prejudice's* younger set:

Mr. Bingley: All the ladies are accomplished. They sing, they draw, they dance, speak French and German, cover screens, and I know not what.

Mr. Darcy: But not half a dozen would satisfy my notion of an accomplished woman.

Miss Bingley: Oh, certainly. No woman can be really esteemed accomplished who does not also possess a certain something in the air, in her manner of walking, in the tone of her voice, her address and expressions.

Mr. Darcy: And to all this she must yet add something more substantial in the improvement of her mind by extensive reading.

Elizabeth Bennet: I'm no longer surprised at you knowing only six accomplished women, Mr. Darcy. I rather wonder at your knowing any.

Ouch.

Language to these people meant more than thoughtless speech or sentiments butchered by dull-edged words. Conversation was an art; words and carefully shaped sentences were jewels, and sometimes weapons. One movie that vividly contrasts this difference in the value of speech is *Possession*, a movie of literary suspense and passion based on A.S. Byatt's novel. Two modern academics seek to discover the nature of the relationship between two long-dead Victorian poets. In cutting back and forth between these two worlds, *Possession* contrasts the speech of the Victorian poets, Randolph Ash and Christabel LaMotte, with their modern counterparts, Roland Mitchell and Maud Bailey. Here, for instance, is a brief exchange between the two Victorian poets in *Possession*:

Randolph Ash: You cut me, Madam.

Christabel LaMotte: I'm sorry. I only meant to scratch.

Contrast these words, or the precise speech of Darcy and Elizabeth, with the twenty-first century scholars, Mitchell and Bailey, as they fall in love in *Possession*.

Roland Mitchell: So what are we gonna do now? We gonna try to beat 'em to France, or—or are we just gonna stare at each other?

Maud Bailey: That is the question, isn't it?

Roland: Mm-hmmm.

Maud: I have one for you.

Roland: What's that?

Maud: What are you really doing here?

Roland: Well, I uh—I needed to see your face. I just wanted to let you know that whatever happened at Whitby, which unfortunately was not much, is not because of anything that you did. Not at all. I just didn't want to jump into something. I mean, I did and I do...want to. Badly. I just didn't want to mess this up. And I just want to see—(clears throat) I want to see if there's an us in you and me. Would—would you like that?

(Maud leans over and kisses Roland)

Roland: I'll take that as a yes.

For the Victorians, and for many other peoples, including those often regarded as primitive, conversation was an art form, clear, beautiful, elegant, and when necessary deadly as a stiletto. For modern romantics, little trained in spoken rhetoric, language becomes more hindrance than help, a thicket to be stumbled through rather than a pathway to the heart.

Possession also offers male viewers insight into some relationship issues of today. Maud Bailey (Gwyneth Paltrow) is an academic whose cool demeanor and flat responses reveal a woman abused emotionally both by men and by feminist colleagues critical of her beauty and long hair, which they regard as overly sexual. As Maud becomes involved with Roland Mitchell (Aaron Eckhart)—they are investigating an exchange of letters and a possible sexual connection between the two Victorian poets—they engage in the erratic steps of our modern-day sexual dance between two adults: the concerns about boundaries, the difficulty in using the word "love," the immense fear of giving away one's heart only to have it returned battered and broken. (Both Paltrow and Eckhart, incidentally, give outstanding performances in this regard.)

As we have seen, one distinguishing mark between chick flicks and action movies is the dialogue. Chick flicks often contain wit and real conversation; action movies focus much more on the physical—car crashes, explosions, fist fights. Women are the ones who encourage men—sometimes strongly—to "express your feelings." Few men would say that to their friends. We are simply not as conversant as women when it comes to sharing our emotions.

Yet we men can take courage from the fact that these movies—and life itself—show us that sincerity, not language, wins hearts. A basic willingness to enter into conversation, which goes by the code word "communication," also counts in establishing a relationship. Being handsome helps attract women, of course, but it's not always necessary. In *Casablanca*, Humphrey Bogart, who had stage presence but never good looks, wins the beautiful Ilsa, and we accept their love as real. Bogart has class and style, and is able to say what he means.

In real life, and even in most movies, women don't want a cringing, whining Woody Allen, a smooth talker, or a Neanderthal.

What they want, as we have said, is a man.

Protect and Defend

The movie has ended, and you are walking toward your car in the mall parking lot with your date, Mollie, who just last week won her black belt in karate. Suddenly a man steps from the shadows. Clearly intoxicated, he curses, raises his fists, and lurches toward you. Do you 1) duck behind Mollie, who is smaller than you but much better trained in hand-to-hand combat or 2) step in front to protect her?

When I ask this question of my male students, they look away from me and shift in their seats. Despite their confusion, I have yet to find one young man who would push the girl in front to face their attacker. They give numerous excuses—"Karate is over-rated," "The dude might be armed," "She's too small"—but most often one of them will blurt out, "Guys just don't do that sort of thing."

Guys don't do that sort of thing.

Men want to protect women just as most women desire and encourage that protection. These mutual and apparently natural desires are a visceral demand from each for strength, assurance, and assistance.

Hollywood recognizes the place of the man as protector and defender. In action and adventure films, in Westerns and detective movies, in dramas and in comedies, in hundreds of films, men protect women from their enemies and defend them against their assailants. Often the woman joins the fight, helping her protector, clobbering a villain or two when her man is down, getting in the face of the bad guys, standing up to injustice.

Kate and Leopold, discussed in the initial chapter of this section, offers two fine examples of such a defense. In the first, Leopold and Kate are walking from her office after he has successfully auditioned to star in one of Kate's commercials. The Victorian Leopold sees one of New York's horse-drawn carriages and asks Kate if she'd like to ride in it, but she hails a taxicab. As she opens the door to enter the cab, a thief snatches her briefcase, leaps a wall into Central Park, and sprints away. Kate follows him, shouting for him to stop, but simply can't keep up.

Kate stops in frustration, then turns at the noise of drumming hooves behind her. It is Leopold, riding the horse from the hack. He takes Kate by the hand, pulls her up behind him, and gives chase to the thief. Within minutes, he corners him against an iron gate beneath a bridge. Swinging a bridle strap, Leopold tells the thief: "I warn you, scoundrel, I was trained at the King's Academy and schooled in weaponry by the palace guard. You stand no chance. When you run, I shall ride; when you stop, the steel of this strap shall be lodged in your brain."

The thief drops the briefcase and flees; the small crowd standing on top of the bridge applauds. As for Kate, she is stunned by Leopold's gallantry and skill.

Later in the movie, Leopold and Charlie, Kate's brother, find Kate and J.J., her boss, sharing a meal at a restaurant. J.J., who has spent the evening trying to impress Kate with his knowledge of wines and opera so as to entice her to sleep with him, is irritated by their intrusion. At one point J.J. tells Leopold that he has invited Kate to see the opera *La Boheme,* from which, he claims, he has learned to speak fluent French, but that Kate has refused his invitation.

J.J.: Leopold, do you enjoy opera?

Leopold: Well, La Boheme is one of man's great achievements and should not be missed, but perhaps Kate resists on moral grounds.

J.J.: How so?

Leopold: Well, some feel that to court a woman in one's employ is nothing more than a serpentine effort to transform a lady into a whore.

J.J.: This guy's charming, Kate. The Duke of Margarine thinks me a serpent.

Kate: No, he doesn't.

Leopold: No, not at serpent. That's too good a word. Simply a braggart and a cad who knows less French than I, if that's possible. (Leopold rises) And by the way, there is no Andre in La Boheme. It's Rodolfo. And though it takes place in France, it's rarely played in French, as it is written in Italian. Good night. (He leaves the restaurant with Charlie in tow).

Here, as we can see, Leopold defends not Kate's property or physical person, but what he regards as her purity.

In *True Grit*, John Wayne stars as Marshall Reuben J. "Rooster" Cogburn. Mattie Ross (Kim Darby), a girl whose father has been murdered, hires Rooster and a Texas ranger, La Boeuf (Glen Campbell) to track down her father's killer. Though Mattie is a tough, independent Presbyterian—"I won't rest until Tom Chaney's barking in hell"—she nonetheless finds herself in need of Rooster's protection, particularly since Chaney has joined up with a gang of outlaws headed by the notorious Ned Pepper (Robert Duvall).

True Grit offers action and sparkling dialogue, with fine performances by Wayne and Darby. In spite of Mattie's own show of grit—she keeps up with Rooster and La Boeuf, and eventually shoots Chaney—the movie shows the necessity for men like Rooster, men on the right side of the law who aren't afraid to run toward danger and the sound of the guns, men who will protect the weak and the innocent.

To Kill A Mockingbird has only one scene in which men physically protect a female. Near the end of the film, Bob Ewell, who has vowed to take vengeance on Atticus for making a fool of him at the trial of a black man, tries to stab Jem's sister Scout (Mary Badham) to death on her way home from a harvest festival. Jem tries to fight off Ewell, but is knocked unconscious. Scout is then rescued by Boo Radley (Robert Duvall), the town misfit who over the years has kept an eye on the children. He stabs Ewell to death and saves Scout's life.

One theme that runs through *To Kill A Mockingbird* is, in fact, our obligation to defend the weak and defenseless. Atticus Finch's defense of Tom Robbins against false charges of assault and rape is unpopular with many of the townspeople, and Scout takes some teasing about it at school, provoking her to fight. In this scene Atticus explains to Scout why he feels compelled to battle for Tom Robbins.

Atticus: There are some things you're not old enough to understand just yet. There's been some high talk around here to the effect that I shouldn't do much about defending this man.

Scout: If you shouldn't be defending him, then why are you doing it?

Atticus: For a number of reasons. The main one is if I didn't, I couldn't hold my head up in town. I couldn't even tell you or Jem not to do something again.

Even a man's most ardent defense of the weak and defenseless can come to failure. In *The Road*, a disturbing film based on Cormac McCarthy's novel by the same name, a great disaster has overtaken humankind. (The book leaves the cause of this disaster cloudy, while the movie hints strongly at an atomic war.) Plants and animals begin dying out, and the surviving human beings become savages, preying on one another and even resorting to cannibalism. The Man (Viggo Mortensen) fails to convince his wife to go on living. Before she kills herself, she tells him she wants to take the Boy with her on her trip to death. The Man refuses to allow her to kill their son, and throughout the remainder of the film he protects the Boy—"I will kill anyone who touches you"—both from the cannibals roaming the highways and from despair. As they make their way south in hopes of finding food and some place to live, the Man again and again reminds the Boy of their mission.

Man: You have to keep carrying the fire.

Boy: What fire?

Man: The fire inside you.

Boy: Are we still the good guys?

Man: Yes, we're still the good guys. Of course we are.

Boy: And always will be? No matter what happens?

Man: Always will.

The Man's love for his son, his determination to see his son survive, and his constant struggles against the elements and the savages who surround them give us a hero, a true defender of the fire.

Family Guys

A Raisin in the Sun, It's a Wonderful Life, The Pursuit of Happyness, To Kill a Mockingbird, A Man for All Seasons: these and other movies shine a light on men and their families. Many such films exist, of course, ranging from light comedies with Dad as a buffoon to dark dramas portraying him as a violent drunkard or an abusive husband and father. While some movies present these husbands and fathers as simplistic, two-dimensional characters, many directors and writers recognize the conflicts men face when balancing their work and their duties outside the home with their obligations to their wives and children.

In *The Great Santini*, for example, a fine underrated film based on the Pat Conroy novel of the same name, Robert Duvall plays Marine Corps fighter pilot Bull Meechum, a savage man who demands the best of himself, his pilots, and his family. He bullies his wife and children, and becomes abusive when drinking, yet clearly values and loves his family. The epitome of an alpha-male, Bull is not the man most of us would want for a father, yet Duvall's performance reveals the complex nature of such a man. He shows us the tension created by coupling a demanding profession to the challenges of family life. Here we see the power and importance of a father in family life, even a father as cruel as Bull Meechum. His wife and children despise his harsh code, but their loyalty to one another and their love for Bull, revealed in the movie's final scenes, provide the frail bindings keeping the family intact.

Perhaps the most powerful examination of family disintegration and ultimate destruction comes to us in in the *Godfather* trilogy. These movies resonate in a profound way with men. Young men are particularly attracted to this story, seeing in the Corleone family and its life of crime certain enviable elements: honor, patriarchy, swift and violent solutions to problems, tangible power, and a code of manhood.

The first movie, *The Godfather*, begins with the wedding of a Mafia boss's daughter. As family and friends celebrate the wedding, this boss—Don Corleone (Marlon Brando), known as the Godfather—remains inside the house in his office, meeting various people who have come to request favors on his daughter's wedding day. It is an old Sicilian custom, and by honoring these obligations to his family and criminal associates, Corleone shows himself a man deeply rooted in Old World traditions. His love of family becomes apparent when he asks his godson, a movie actor who has come to him for a favor, "Tell me, do you spend time with your family?...Because a man who doesn't spend time with his family is not a real man." This advice is aimed not only at his godson, but also at Corleone's eldest son, Sonny (James Caan), who has just stepped into the office after cheating on his wife.

When the old man is later gunned down by some of his rivals—he survives the attempted murder, but is badly wounded—we see the beginnings of the disintegration of the Corleone family. Sonny, a hotheaded man with no sense of his father's finesse, is killed in the gang war; Don Corleone's youngest son Michael (Al Pacino) avenges these hits on his father and brother, but is forced to flee to Sicily. By the movie's end, Michael has returned to New York and becomes the head of the Corleone family. He marries his lover, Kay Adams (Diane Keaton), with the promise that he will steer the Corleone family into legitimate business.

Yet in the final scene, we see Michael through Kay's eyes as he stands like an ancient Roman emperor in his father's office with his henchmen kissing his hand. Slowly Michael's bodyguard closes the door on Kay, separating her from "the family".

Throughout the three movies, Michael Corleone symbolizes the destruction of the family. By the time the third movie ends, he has become a withered man on the cusp of old age, a murderer whose victims include his own brother, divorced by his wife, despised by his sister, the father of a murdered daughter, and the godfather of a Mafia family no longer operating by a code of honor. Even his diminished physical stature—the tall young soldier returned from the war in the Pacific is now small and frail—reveals his broken life and the absence of the code practiced by his father. Michael Corleone has defeated all of his enemies except himself.

The Godfather trilogy offers us, especially through Michael, much to contemplate on the subject of manhood. With the gravity and depth of a Greek tragedy, it relates a story in which, like the plays of Sophocles, the hero is swept by circumstance and passion into a destiny not of his own making. Like Oedipus, like Cleon, Michael Corleone is a victim of fate, a man who starts down what he regards as the right path in life but who cannot see, until it is too late, the turnings of that path and the pain that such a journey will bring him. Michael's efforts to serve and save his family produce in the end only a litter of bodies, broken promises, and dreams twisted into nightmares.

Standing in contrast to *The Godfather* as a portrait of family values is Andrew McLaglen's *Shenandoah*. Here Charlie Anderson (Jimmy Stewart) acts, as does Don Corleone, as a protector of his family. Here too, as in *The Godfather*, a tension exists between that immediate family and the outside forces threatening it. This time, however, the forces that Anderson must battle are war and government rather than a monster of his own creation.

Charlie Anderson is a farmer in Virginia's Shenandoah Valley, an independent man who attempts to protect his family from the ravages of the Civil War and from the intrusions of the armies of both the North and the South. A widower deeply devoted to his children, all but one of whom is fully grown, Anderson represents an earlier America that regarded the individual as superior to the state. At one point, a recruiting officer named Johnson tells him he is wrong to keep his sons on the farm when the army so desperately needs men:

Anderson: Can you give me one good reason why I should let my sons march down that road like a bunch of damn fools?

Lt. Johnson: Virginia needs all her sons, Mr. Anderson.

Anderson: They don't belong to the state. They belong to ME! When they were babies I never saw the state coming around here with a spare tit!

Despite his best efforts, Anderson and his sons become embroiled in the conflict. His youngest son, Boy (Philip Alford), finds a Confederate cap in the woods, puts it on his head, and is then picked up as a soldier by a Union patrol. Accompanied by his daughter, Jennie (Rosemary Forsyth), and by all but one of his sons, Anderson sets out to rescue Boy. A series of calamities befalls them. In their absence, the son who has remained at home on the farm is murdered along with his wife by marauders, and a Confederate sentry accidentally kills another one of Anderson's sons, Jacob (Glenn Corbett). They do find Jennie's husband, a Confederate army officer, among a group of prisoners and forcibly gain his release, but then, shattered by their ordeal, they return home without Boy. At the end of the film, Boy, who had escaped from the Union Army only to be thrown into fighting for the Confederates, finally rejoins the family during a Sunday worship service, limping into the church on crutches from a crippling wound to his leg.

Like Don Corleone, Charlie Anderson lives by a code of honor that almost breaks him. Unlike Don Corleone, his code is worthy of his fight. He places his family above the state; he values hard work, honesty, and love; he turns a granite face to the outside world, but tenders a soft heart toward his daughter and sons. When he visits the grave of his wife, Martha, and speaks to her of his difficulties in raising their children, we come to understand that he remains deeply in love with her. Her influence is responsible for the family's attendance at church and its mealtime prayers. "Now," says Charlie Anderson at one point, "your mother wanted you all raised as good Christians, and I may not be able to do that thorny job as well as she could, but I can do something about your manners." By the movie's end, we are aware that the love between Charlie and Martha, and his abiding affection for her even sixteen years after her death, have built a throne of love among his children. We are left only to wonder whether Charlie himself might have become such a hardened case had Martha lived to grow old beside him.

Once again we can see the value of a code in a man's life. Charlie loved Martha in life and honored her in death. In *Shenandoah* we have yet another reminder, had we need of one, that the vows made at a wedding—to love, honor, and cherish—are the foundation stones of true love and marriage.

Part IV
Men and God

You came to see a race today. To see someone win. It happened to be me. But I want you to do more than just watch a race. I want you to take part in it. I want to compare faith to running in a race. It's hard. It requires concentration, energy of the soul. You experience elation when the winner breaks the tape—especially if you've got a bet on it. But how long does it last? You go home. Maybe your dinner's burnt. Maybe you haven't got a job. So who am I to say, "Believe, have faith," in the face of life's realities? I would like to give you something more permanent, but I can only point the way. I have no formula for winning the race. Everyone runs in her own way, or his own way. And where does this power come from, to see the race to its end? From within.

—Eric Liddell in *Chariots of Fire*

I'm forever in pursuit and I don't even know what I'm chasing.

—Harold Abrahams in *Chariots of Fire*

The Hidden God

Many Americans profess a belief in some sort of deity. Even those who claim atheism as the banner of their faith must believe in something: a cause, a philosophy, some branch of science, the self. To believe in nothing, to lack faith of any kind, would surely mark the death of our humanity.

Faith in God by its very nature implies a leap beyond reason, beyond the tangible, beyond the physical world of the senses. Whatever our faith, whether we believe in the existentialism of Sartre or the sociobiology of E.O. Wilson, whether we spend our Saturdays in a temple or our Sundays in a church, we are following a trail whose physical evidence only extends so far before faith and imagination begin to guide our steps.

What we believe, and just as importantly, how fervently we adhere to our beliefs, may deeply determine the course of this trail, this pilgrimage that in so many ways constitutes our very life. The Christian who attends church a few times a year, who prays only in moments of crisis, and who follows his own whims regarding moral choices is perhaps no poorer for his practices than the daily Mass attendee, if the latter does not put faith into practice. "Faith without works is dead," says the Old Book, and this adage holds true whether the believer is a Christian or an agnostic, a Mormon or a Buddhist. To fail to practice our faith leads to spiritual death.

When we are growing to manhood, we may search in many places before we find a place to call home. The Christian raised in an evangelical household may find himself as an adult seeking to deepen his faith in an ashram in Wyoming; the secular Jew who spent his teenage years celebrating only the high holy days may someday find his home among the Orthodox. From a forge and hammer made of books, classes, encounters with people and ideas, and our own experiences, we beat out a faith by which we can make our way in the world.

Movies can help shape our faith. They can act as guides on our expedition. It is true that certain movies attack religious faith, particularly Christianity, and social conservatives in particular have condemned these films for their bias and their deceits. Films like *Monsignor*, *The Da Vinci Code*, and *The Last Temptation of Christ* seem clearly intended as assaults on Christianity.

Yet many Hollywood films explore belief and faith in God with honesty and sincerity. In fact, nearly all the films reviewed in this book shine a light, at one moment or another, on some aspect of religion and faith. Directors, producers, and writers of films are no different than the rest of us in seeking spiritual values.

Then where, some may ask, are the religious pictures? Where are the pictures like those made in an earlier era: *The Robe*, *The Bells of Saint Mary's*, *Angels With Dirty Faces*, *Ben Hur*?

The answer to this question is simple: films with religious themes are still very much with us. The difference between the films of today and those earlier movies is one of degree and subtlety. Directors and writers now frequently hide religion and God within the picture, embedding such themes, often deeply, in a film, both for artistic and commercial reasons. Too often it is we viewers who, whether from sloth or critical blindness, fail to grasp these hidden meanings, yet they are readily available to the observant viewer.

A majority of the films reviewed here, as I said earlier, touch at times on faith and God. *Groundhog Day* gives us a man being perfected by an external force some critics equate with God. *Tender Mercies* appears on its face as the story of a country singer fallen on hard times, yet it is filled with allusions to God and Christianity. Numerous movies display religious symbolism—a crucifix on a bedroom wall, actresses wearing a cross or crucifix. In *Cool Hand Luke*, Luke pretends to speak with God, lies on a table as if bound to a cross after winning an egg-eating contest, and several times undergoes his punishment and suffering with old-time hymns being played in the background. Even a movie like Whit Stillman's *The Last Days of Disco*, so seemingly concerned with the mores and beliefs of the late 1970s, conceals beneath its often-comic exterior an awareness of the value of spirit and faith. One of the main characters, a lawyer with the strongest conscience of his disco friends, sings the lines of an old hymn to the woman he loves. He sings so softly that many viewers doubtless miss the implications of this scene.

In his Rocky pictures, director Sylvester Stallone blends the boxer's religious faith into the movie so well that it can be easily overlooked. These films never beat us over the head with Rocky's Catholic faith, but we are treated in each movie to the spectacle of a man who, engaged in some struggle, still prays and is clearly a believer. From the scene in *Rocky II*, when Rocky prays for Adrian in the hospital chapel, to the humorous scene in *Rocky Balboa*, when Spider Rico, once Rocky's opponent, insists on washing the dishes in Rocky's restaurant because Jesus has told him to do so, Stallone permits us quick insights into the spiritual life of his characters.

We can no longer expect characters like Bing Crosby in *The Bells of Saint Mary's*. Moviemakers who wish to include religious themes recognize they must be subtle if they wish to attract a large audience. If we know how to look, however, we will find God and man confronting each other on the big screen.

Faith of Our Fathers

Young men who attend religious services sometimes gain the impression that religion and spirituality have become the province of the female. Though the celebrant of the religious ceremony—a priest, pastor, rabbi—may be male, women operate most of the other offices and ministries within the institutional church. Even more importantly, from the male perspective, the language, thought, and conduct of present-day religious ceremony bear a strong feminine stamp. The language of the twenty-first century religious service is couched in the language of women and the therapeutic society. Among Christians, for example, Christ these days is less King, Judge, or Master than he is Healer, Friend, and Comforter. (One glaring exception to this argument may be found in the Shrine of the Immaculate Conception in Washington, D.C. Here on the ceiling above the central altar is an enormous mosaic of a stern, muscular Christ, clearly macho, clearly taking into judgment those who view him. His appearance shocks many modern day visitors. Designed in the middle part of the twentieth century, this powerful masculine image of Christ contradicts the saccharine Jesus touted by so many contemporary worshippers.)

Church music reinforces this feminization. "Onward Christian Soldiers" has given way to "Let Us Break Bread Together on Our Knees," "A Mighty Fortress is Our God" to "Let There Be Peace on Earth." On the radio, many Christian pop bands play and sing cloying music few young men could possibly love. Even the pitch at which such music is sung rarely offers the bass voice a part.

Movies reflect this trend. Often writers and directors portray male pastors—and hence God—as phony, weak, or even evil. *Going My Way* and *Angels With Dirty Faces* have given way to *Godfather III* and *The Da-Vinci Code*. To underscore this point, we need only turn to the film *Zulu*, which tells the story of the battle between English soldiers and Zulu warriors at Rorke's Drift. *Zulu* paints the chaplain of this heroic stand as a drunk and a coward. In reality, the chaplain at Rorke's Drift was commended for his actions in battle. Most faithful moviegoers can easily count a dozen films in which Catholic priests and Protestant ministers are portrayed as corrupt criminals, swindlers, child molesters, liars, connivers, and scoundrels.

Yet there are movies in which religion and pastors are presented sympathetically, and from which young men may draw both inspiration and manly lessons.

In Elia Kazan's *On The Waterfront*, Karl Malden plays Father Barry, a Catholic priest in a working-class neighborhood in Brooklyn who finds himself battling the corrupt union that controls the nearby docks. This priest calls together a handful of workers willing to fight the unions and, after listening to their grievances, promises them he will go the last mile with them in their struggle against corruption. When one of these workers, Kayo Dugan, is murdered while unloading a ship, Father Barry goes down to the docks and, standing over Kayo's corpse, delivers a speech condemning the union leaders. Here is a part of that speech, one of the finest of its kind in the history of Hollywood:

"Some people think the crucifixion only took place on Calvary. They better wise up! Taking Joey Doyle's life to stop him from testifying is a crucifixion. And dropping a sling on Kayo Dugan because he was ready to spill his guts tomorrow, that's a crucifixion. And every time the Mob puts the pressure on a good man, tries to stop him from doing his duty as a citizen, it's a crucifixion. And anybody

who sits around and lets it happen, keeps silent about something he knows that happened, shares the guilt of it just as much as the Roman soldier who pierced the flesh of our Lord to see if he was dead."

Father Barry fulfills his promise: he stays involved in the fight against union gangsterism and helps inspire Terry Malloy (Marlon Brando) to join the cause and stand against corruption.

Agnieszka Holland's *The Third Miracle* examines doubting priest Father Frank Shore (Ed Harris), a man in desperate search of some outward sign of God's existence. He has the chance to pursue this quest when his bishop orders him to investigate a statue of Mary weeping blood in a church schoolyard. Here he discovers a connection between the statue and a woman, Helen, who may have died a saint.

During the investigation, he becomes strongly attracted to Helen's daughter, Roxane (Anne Heche). After a short torrid flirtation, they are in each other's arms and on their way to the bedroom when it begins raining (the statue bleeds only in November and only when it rains). Promising he'll return as soon as possible, Frank rushes off to the church, where he learns that the statue is indeed weeping tears of human blood. This realization renews his faith and changes his life, and he spends the rest of the movie defending Helen's cause for sainthood.

Though saints and bleeding statues are not to everyone's taste, *The Third Miracle* makes some important points. For one, it allows us to watch a priest, the son of a Chicago cop and a tough man himself, wrestling with his faith. In contrast to his friend Father John Leone (Michael Rispoli), who tells Frank at one point that he has never questioned his faith, Frank struggles against a tempestuous sea of doubts and black despair. He drinks too much booze, gives way to sexual temptation, and nearly abandons the priesthood. Once he realizes the reality of the miracle, however, he finds a cause worthy of his love and energy, and remains true to his vocation as a priest.

Of course, not all who struggled with their faith will receive such proof positive of the miraculous. The real point to *The Third Miracle* comes not with the realization of the miracle, but with Father Frank's defense of the miracle and Helen's sainthood when he faces an investigator from the Vatican. When this investigator accuses Father Frank of being weak in his faith, the priest acknowledges his wounded interior life and his unworthiness to defend the cause of Helen, yet he perseveres in his fight for Helen, certain now that she is a saint and with God. Fighting these battles on Helen's behalf eventually makes Father Frank a strong priest. For believers, this movie tells us that our struggles to believe, however painful and arduous, are winnable and may contain miracles and hidden rewards of their own.

Though his stock is low among believers, a religious motif runs through the movies of Woody Allen. Even in his comedies, he often touches, however lightly, on religious themes: the nature of divinity, the place of God in our lives, the meaning of good and evil.

In *Crimes and Misdemeanors*, which is his most thoughtful film on good and evil, Allen more openly analyzes both the nature of God and our relationship to a divine power. This film also raises some of Plato's ideas on justice found in *The Republic*, specifically his account of the gold ring of Gyges, a shepherd who discovers a ring that brings invisibility to its wearer. Using Gyges as his model, Plato philosophizes on the nature of justice and whether men voluntarily follow the path of righteousness. Given such invisibility, he asks, would men behave in a moral way toward their fellow creatures? Would they not instead use the ring for thievery, rape, murder, and other heinous crimes?

Crimes and Misdemeanors tells the story of six men and their relation to God and to others around them. As Cliff Stern, Woody Allen plays his usual role as a whiny neurotic. Here he is a film director interested in making documentaries who is forced by financial circumstances to work for his brother-in-law and film director, Lester (Alan Alda), a pretentious snob, but also a man who knows how to make films.

The heart of the movie revolves around three men linked together by their knowledge of an act of adultery and murder. Judah Rosenthal (Martin Landau), a famous surgeon, has a mistress, Dolores Paley

(Anjelica Huston), who recklessly threatens to expose their affair unless he leaves his wife and marries her. Judah confesses the affair and the threats made by Dolores to Ben (Sam Waterston), a rabbi who is losing his sight. Ben gently counsels Judah to tell his wife everything about Dolores and the affair, certain this revelation will produce forgiveness from his wife and redemption for Judah. Feeling, however, that this confession would destroy his marriage, Judah turns next to his brother Jack (Jerry Orbach), a thug and a criminal who promises Judah he can arrange for the elimination of Dolores. Though Judah initially refuses Jack's offer, eventually he gives his approval, and Jack has Dolores murdered.

A sixth man acts as a kind of Greek chorus in *Crimes and Misdemeanors*. This is Professor Levy (Martin S. Bergmann), whom we meet only through the documentary Cliff is making about him. At one point we hear Professor Levy telling the camera:

"We're all faced throughout our lives with agonizing decisions, moral choices. Some are on a grand scale; most of these choices are on lesser points. But we define ourselves by the choices we have made. We are, in fact, the sum total of our choices. Events unfold so unpredictably, so unfairly, human happiness does not seem to be included in the design of creation. And yet, most human beings seem to have the ability to keep trying and even to find joy from simple things, like their family, their work, and from the hope that future generations might understand more."

As each of these men struggles with moral dilemmas, some of which bear profound consequences, the question of God enters into the film.

Judah: I remember my father telling me, "The eyes of God are on us always." The eyes of God. What a phrase to a young boy. What were God's eyes like? Unimaginably penetrating, intense eyes, I assumed. And I wonder if it was just a coincidence that made my specialty ophthalmology.

Sight and blindness are a key theme to *Crimes and Misdemeanors*. Judah is an ophthalmologist, yet he slowly becomes morally blind; Ben is going blind, sinking into a world of darkness, yet he lives in a world of light when compared to Judah.

Ben: It's a human life. You don't think God sees?

Judah: God is a luxury I can't afford.

Judah resembles so many human beings today, especially those who believe in God and morality, who pick and choose what laws they wish to obey in that moral framework. They are cafeteria believers, accepting doctrines of faith pleasing to them, rejecting those they regard as too demanding. This idea comes clear in another part of dialogue where Judah says to Ben: "Jack lives in the real world. You live in the kingdom of heaven. I'd managed to keep free of that real world but suddenly it's found me."

Uttering these words, Judah sounds not tough but pathetic. He is a grown man, a man highly respected for his surgical skills and his generosity. Yet it is Judah who has initiated the affair with Dolores, who continues to see Dolores, who is too weak to tell his wife the truth, but resorts instead to paid murder. The "real world" doesn't find him; he creates the ugly dilemma in which he finds himself.

At the end of the movie, at a party, Judah and Cliff happen to meet alone outside. Here Judah, learning that Cliff is a filmmaker, asks if he might tell him a story. He tells Cliff the story would make a great movie, but in actuality he describes his own life—the affair, the threats by the man's mistress, her subsequent murder. After finishing the story, Judah says:

"And after the awful deed is done, he finds that he is plagued by deep-rooted guilt. Little sparks of his religious background, which he'd rejected, are suddenly stirred up. He hears his father's voice. He imagines that God is watching his every move. Suddenly, it's not an empty universe at all, but a just and moral one, and he's violated it. Now, he's panic-stricken. He's on the verge of a mental collapse—an

inch away from confessing the whole thing to the police. And then one morning, he awakens. The sun is shining, his family is around him and mysteriously, the crisis has lifted. He takes his family on vacation to Europe and as the months pass, he finds he's not punished. In fact, he prospers. The killing gets attributed to another person—a drifter who has a number of other murders to his credit, so I mean, what the hell? One more doesn't even matter. Now he's scot-free. His life is completely back to normal. Back to his protected world of wealth."

Judah then contends that this is the way the movie should realistically end, with right overturned and evil in the saddle. And this is, indeed, the way *Crimes and Misdemeanors* does end.

Some reviewers have attacked the moral premises of this movie, largely on the basis of Judah's seemingly triumphant evil. Yet they miss, I think, Woody Allen's key idea behind the film, which is not that evil is triumphant but whether God exists. If God does exist and sees all things, then Judah's punishment will be carried out in the next world. If God does not exist, then yes, Judah has escaped punishment, but he has also overturned the natural law: Thou shalt not kill. He has wounded what C.S. Lewis called the Way, the law common to nearly all societies and religions on earth.

Judah may have escaped the punishment of the law, but often the Way has a way—pardon the pun—of catching up with its violators. The fact that Judah feels compelled to confess to Allen, that he has to excuse his murder, tells us he is no longer the man of honor and good spirit shown at the beginning of the film.

He has, quite literally, lost his way.

Foxholes

"There are no atheists in foxholes:" so the old adage runs. Judging from accounts of American military action in Vietnam, Iraq, and Afghanistan, modern soldiers share the anxieties and fears of earlier generations in battle, though they also may share the diminished religious faith of their countrymen. Polls indicate that we Americans are less religiously cohesive than ever before, and fewer American Christians attend Sunday services than they did in 1950—in terms of percentages, that is. And yet the great majority of citizens claim to believe in a personal God and an afterlife. Often this faith, whether fervent or lackadaisical, may amble along untested for long periods of time.

War, however, is a crucible that does test the faith of men. Beyond all other human endeavors, war intensifies the emotions and experiences of its participants. Modern warfare throws together a gaggle of strangers and binds them into a brotherhood tighter than that of any college fraternity. For the front-line soldier in particular, little has changed in that regard since Homer wrote the *Iliad*. Death, killing, privation, fear, and suffering remain the soldier's boon companions. He depends on the man to his left and to his right to achieve victory and to survive defeat.

War is also the one activity left to our society dominated by males. It is true that women today play military roles unimagined by their great-grandmothers: serving in front-line capacities, flying combat aircraft, operating in all visible ways as soldiers. Yet the casualty lists from battles of the last sixty years and the predominance of men today in outfits like the Rangers, the Special Forces, and Marine Recon stake out the battlefield as a male preserve, a killing ground where men generally reveal their heroism or cowardice, their compassion or their cruelty, without female influence.

Like its audience, Hollywood is fascinated by war and its effects on men. Moviemakers recognize that combat provides a dramatic opportunity for the study of character. They understand that the battlefield acts as a testing ground for young men, a rite of passage into manhood. From *The Deer Hunter* to *Platoon*, from *The Patriot* to *Black Hawk Down*, Hollywood has produced films exhibiting its interest in men at war.

Frequently in these films Hollywood looks at the effects of combat on the faith of the young who do battle. Once again, as in so many films made today, the writers and directors who seek a wide audience approach faith and religion with subtlety.

In *Saving Private Ryan*, the story of D-Day, the landing at Utah Beach, and the fighting in the week following the invasion, director Steven Spielberg shows us soldiers on the beach praying as they lie wounded or charge toward the enemy. Some make the sign of the cross before going into battle, others pray the rosary on the embattled beach, and the dying receive last rites from a priest.

One of the main characters, Daniel Jackson (Barry Pepper), is a sniper who, like Alvin York in the First World War, prays before shooting at the enemy, reciting scripture and asking God to make his aim true. The movie makes little comment, positive or negative, on Jackson's faith; his prayers are presented as naturally as the cursing of some of the other men. Jackson does, however, remain an enigma to some of his fellow soldiers. Once, when the squad hunkers down for the night inside a battered church and Jackson falls into a deep sleep, two soldiers discuss Jackson's ability to sleep under such circumstances. "A clear conscience," one of them says. These soldiers have missed the point: Jackson sleeps well not because of a clear conscience but because of his faith. He has placed himself in the hands of his god. Whatever the outcome of battle, Jackson gives us the impression that he takes comfort in the saving grace of that god. Here the director has achieved a truth overlooked by many other war films, that worship and faith play an integral part in the lives of many men facing death on the battlefield. God is not left at home along with Mom and apple pie.

In *Heaven Knows, Mr. Allison*, John Huston's picture about the Second World War in the Pacific, Marine Corporal Allison (Robert Mitchum) washes up on the shore of a small Pacific Island after the Japanese sink his ship. Here he meets Sister Angela (Deborah Kerr), a nun left behind in the small mission on the island. Though raised Catholic, Mr. Allison, as the sister calls him, is not particularly devout. His devotion is to the Marine Corps, which he compares favorably to Sister Angela's religious order. When the Japanese land, Corporal Allison protects the sister. He helps her hide in a cave, steals food from the Japanese, and is prepared to die in her defense. At one point in the movie, however, he becomes drunk and makes advances toward her. She flees the cave and becomes ill after spending the night in the rain. Corporal Allison finds her and nurses her back to health, stealing medicine from the enemy and killing a Japanese soldier during his raid on their camp.

In Corporal Allison we see the effect of faith on a man who has grown up hard and has spent years in the company of other hardened men. He watches bemused as Sister Angela offers her evening prayers, asks her about her religious life, and comes to respect her fortitude and her dependence on God. By the end of *Heaven Knows, Mr. Allison*, we are led to believe that Corporal Allison's exposure to Sister Angela's faith will lead him back to God as well.

Tears of the Sun in some ways resembles *Heaven Knows, Mr. Allison*, in that it contrasts the military virtues of duty and obedience with the faith of a woman determined to fulfill her obligations. Lieutenant A.K. Waters (Bruce Willis) and his men are assigned the task of removing a priest, two nuns, and a French physician, Dr. Lena Kendricks (Monica

Bellucci), from a vicious civil war in sub-Saharan Africa. Waters rescues Kendricks, though he leaves behind the people in her charge to their certain death. Once he witnesses the murder of the priest, nuns, and other innocents, Waters, disobeying orders, turns the helicopter around and returns to those he has abandoned.

Tears of the Sun is by no means as overtly religious as *Heaven Knows, Mr. Allison*, yet we see the play of faith in the lives of both the fugitives and the soldiers. One of the nuns remains with the ill and wounded of the village, knowing she will die. Several of the fugitives reveal their Christianity to their military rescuers. Though primarily men of violence—and these are men, not boys—we can once again see how faith and innocence can inspire hardened warriors to heroic deeds.

Gods and Generals, Ronald F. Maxwell's prequel to Gettysburg, makes no bones about the place of prayer and worship in the lives of those who fought in the Civil War. Deliberately slow in its plotting—the director's attempts to recreate the feel of small wartime Southern towns cost him much in the face of an audience used to action pictures—*Gods and Generals* is perhaps the only movie ever made in which the viewer might humorously remark that there was too much prayer.

The story focuses on Stonewall Jackson (Stephen Lang), a great commander and a man of deep faith. He constantly invokes the name of the Lord, prays often, and clearly lets his beliefs guide his daily life. When asked by an officer how he can remain so calm in the face of the enemy, Jackson replies: "Mr. Smith, my religious faith teaches me that God has already fixed the time of my death; therefore, I think not of it. I am as calm in battle as I would be in my own parlor. God will come for me in his own time."

Some modern viewers may be put off by Jackson's invocations of the Almighty, yet Maxwell has given us an accurate picture of the general whom many of that time, and later, regarded as an American Cromwell. (Cromwell was the Calvinist general who defeated the king in the English Civil War.) Prayer was as natural to Jackson, and to many of his fellow soldiers in both armies, as breathing. To these soldiers, who fought and died only seven generations ago, a real man carried his faith close to his heart, taking from it courage and compassion.

One director in particular has looked hard at the connections between faith and war. Mel Gibson, who has roiled the waters of controversy in the last twenty years—the media have, at various times, dubbed him a drunk, an anti-Semite, a religious fanatic, a man abusive in some personal relationships—nonetheless recognizes in his movies the importance of faith.

In *Braveheart*, Gibson's movie about William Wallace and the struggle for Scottish independence from England, we see in many small scenes acts of faith performed by the Scottish rebels. After William Wallace's father is buried—he died fighting the English— his uncle asks the young Wallace whether the Mass was in Latin and what the priest said. Later, when Wallace (Mel Gibson) returns to his highland home and marries Murron (Catherine McCormack), the girl he has loved since he was young, the movie shows them kneeling before a priest during the marriage ceremony. Before the battle in which Wallace first defeats the English, his men kneel in their ranks and receive a blessing from a priest. Throughout the picture, we have the impression that Wallace is a man of God, a warrior who depends on his faith in battle and political intrigue.

In Randall Wallace's *We Were Soldiers Once...And Young*, Gibson plays Lieutenant-Colonel Hal Moore, who led his troops in the first pitched battle between American troops and North Vietnamese regulars. Here again the director reveals the importance of faith to a soldier and to men in general. Before he is sent overseas, we see Hal Moore praying at night with his children and discussing with them the efficacy of prayer. One of his officers, Lieutenant Jack Geoghegan (Chris Klein), a young man of deep faith who has fears that he won't return from Vietnam to his family or will somehow fail in his duty, approaches Moore with his concerns, and the two of them go into the chapel to meditate and to pray for God's will in their lives. Later, after Geoghegan dies on the field of battle, Moore writes a letter to the lieutenant's wife in which he says:

"But I know he is with God and the angels now, and I know even Heaven is improved by his presence." On the battlefield itself, we witness Moore praying over his fallen soldiers.

All of these movies point to the centrality of faith in men of action. Despite protests that Hollywood either ignores or attacks religious belief, these films remind viewers of the power of faith in the lives of men. They in fact urge us, by way of example, to practice that faith. For careful observers, these movies make clear that faith does not diminish or weaken us, that it is not only for women and children, that it is not some false hope to which only the cowardly and the weak cling.

Such faith is not made only for the carnage and death of war. Life itself is a battlefield. It brings its own stresses, its casualties, its victories and defeats. Young men in particular should seek out faith, guided in part by their parents, mentors, and teachings from the past, and in part by their own inclination to know the truth of things. Faith, some say, is a gift, but it is a gift that can be won, a precious gift that can be ours if we pursue it hard enough and endure in that pursuit.

A strong faith makes for strong men.

Searchers and Sojourners

As we awake from childhood and walk into adolescence and then into our adult selves, many of us become aware of an emptiness within our hearts, a tiny place, no bigger than the mustard seed of the parable, that often grows as we grow. Caught up in the diversions of youth—sports, academics, the excitement and stress of transitioning into the world at large—we often remain unaware of this tiny void within ourselves. Even if we are conscious of its presence, we may fail to examine or ponder its implications. In his short stories, Ernest Hemingway identifies this hole as a nothingness, as "nada", and tells his readers the best solution is not to think about it, to engage the world but not to think about the widening hollow place within the heart.

Like Hemingway's characters, many young men try to patch this hole with pleasures of the world—sports and friends when younger, sex, drugs, booze, and money making when older. For a time these patches may work, particularly if the practitioners follow Hemingway's advice not to think too hard. Too often, however, these patches fail, and the consequences can be dire, ranging from high rates of suicide among some vulnerable young men to the aimless approach to life taken by so many others.

Others are more successful—at least, on the surface. They patch up these spiritual conflicts and questions—Who am I? What am I? Why am I here?—and push them aside until late in life, even unto the point of death. Here the most addictive drug for our spiritual condition is modernity itself. Our world of gadgets and technology induces spiritual slumber while our hectic schedules wrap us in a cocoon of work, friends, and obligations that anesthetize our questing selves, putting to bed the vital questions regarding existence and our reason for being.

Eventually, of course, a shipwreck shakes us from our slumber. The death of a loved one, the betrayal of a close friend, a divorce, the smashing up of all our ambitions, a crash from addiction or pleasure: these circumstances toss us into the sea, where we flail about looking for some solid piece of ground, some clod of earth on which to stand again.

Alcoholics Anonymous, one of the great social programs of the last century, recognizes that addiction to alcohol occurs in part because addicts lack a central philosophy that might guide their lives. AA refers to this philosophy as a "higher power." The men and women who first directed the organization understood that human beings need something beyond temporary pleasures and solaces—in this case, alcohol—to find fulfillment in life. They realized we fall prey to calamity in part because of what we believe—or don't believe. Even the man who has a plan, who attacks the world with the intention of becoming rich or powerful, who sacrifices much of himself in that attack, will ultimately fail if he has no underlying philosophy as a guide. Each new objective conquered will seem empty to him; each race won leads only to another race. Fame, wealth, and power count for much in the world, but these things turn to dust unless we gain them for some reason other than personal gratification. The recognition of that truth can often bring the best of us crashing to our knees.

Following what many philosophers and spiritual masters have described as "The Way" does not guarantee a life without struggle. If anything, to follow the path of Christ, the Buddha, the Stoics, or any other such guide to life, almost inevitably makes living more difficult.

Here I will inject a personal note. For the first eighteen years of my life, I was a nominal Protestant. My family attended church, prayed at meals, and on rare occasions discussed religious faith. For the next twenty years, I might best be described as an agnostic in search of answers. My gods, if I had any, were the writers I admired, and my churches were libraries or bookstores.

Since the age of 40, I have lived as a believing Roman Catholic. This is not the time or place to discuss my conversion, but I do wish to note that after my honeymoon with the Church, I still find myself struggling to embrace a Christian life. I make mistakes, I fall on my face, I sin. Yet the difference between my self at age thirty and my self today is profound. The code by which I try to live is now set on a firm foundation.

Louis Malle's *My Dinner With Andre* examines this quest for faith. Andre Gregory is a director of plays who has suffered an emotional breakdown of sorts and has recently returned to Manhattan after a long absence abroad. Wally Shawn is his friend, an actor and playwright whom Gregory has invited to dinner. Gregory dominates their conversation through most of the movie, relating to Shawn his search for spiritual truth in exotic locales. By exposing himself to various gurus and bizarre experiences, Gregory hoped to find some meaning in his life beyond his family and the world of the theater.

In the final third of the film, Shawn begins responding to Gregory, telling his friend that he himself doesn't need to indulge in such wild adventures to discover himself. Shawn explains to Gregory—and the audience—that he enjoys his daily routine and finds pleasures in even small acts: conversations with his girlfriend, a cup of coffee in the morning, writing his minor plays. The two men argue amicably over the meaning of life and the ways in which a man can best engage the world.

My Dinner With Andre is an unusual movie. Both actors essentially play themselves, and the only other speakers are the bartender and the waiter in the restaurant. Some viewers will find the movie disconcerting—the entire action takes place through conversation—and will be tempted to abandon the film.

Such a cursory dismissal would be unfortunate, for *My Dinner With Andre* has much to tell us about men and their spiritual needs and desires. Gregory is the man of passion, of feeling, a romantic who has charged headlong into his quest to uncover the meaning of his own existence. From his experiences and teachings, Gregory draws two conclusions: the modern world is somehow sick, and he has discovered no real answers to the questions that prompted his search in the first place. Shawn, the rational man who lacks Gregory's wealth and so must work harder for a living, rebuts his friend's mysticism and his assertions regarding the ills of technology and the emptiness of life, yet he offers few answers to the questions raised by Gregory.

Strangely, what is absent from the ninety minute discussion of these two men is any real mention of God, that Higher Power in which most of the human race believe. Gregory dwells on manifestations of the spiritual and on possible miracles, but never goes beyond these outward signs, while the skeptical Shawn seems to dismiss religious faith entirely. Both men belong to a post-modernist culture in which God is no longer sought as an answer to spiritual dilemmas.

"When people stop believing in God," wrote G.K. Chesterton, "they don't believe in nothing—they believe in anything." *My Dinner With Andre* stands, perhaps unintentionally, as a strong verification of Chesterton's adage. Both Gregory and Shawn represent the turning-inward of post-modern man, seeking "god" within the confines of personal experience. Gregory's willingness to leap at the wildest of ideas—that New York City is a prison in which the natives have incarcerated themselves, that the world of culture and ideas is at a dead-end, that diseases can be cured solely by our thoughts—shows us a man picking up new philosophies like a customer in a cafeteria. The movie may provide few answers for living, but it does an extraordinary job of reflecting the confusion of spiritual ideas in the twenty-first century.

Chariots Of Fire gives us a different picture of spiritual struggle. The characters of Eric Liddell (Ian Charleson) and Harold Abrahams (Ben Cross) are based on two British athletes who competed in the 1924 Summer Olympics. Abrahams, a Jewish student at Cambridge, uses the track as the means to fight anti-Semitism; Liddell uses his own running as a way of honoring God. He tells his sister he can feel God's strength in him when he runs and implies that running therefore reflects the glory of God. We observe him giving witness several times to his faith—see the quotations at the beginning of Part IV—and soon realize he is sincere in his beliefs.

When Liddell discovers that the Olympic committee has scheduled his event for a Sunday, his faith faces a severe test. Believing the Sabbath should be set aside as a day of worship and reflection—earlier in the movie he rebukes some boys for playing games on Sunday—Liddell refuses to participate in the race, even under royal pressure. "God made countries," he says in the film. "God made kings, and the rules by which they govern. And those rules say the Sabbath is His. And I for one intend to keep it that way."

After a teammate switches events with him, Liddell, who twenty years later would die a missionary in a Japanese prison camp, does run and wins an Olympic gold medal. What he represents for us is not the man searching for his religious faith—he clearly owns that—but the man who must stand by his faith. This struggle is familiar to anyone who tries to abide by their faith while at the same time confronting the demands and temptations of the world. Liddell's struggle is a reminder of the cost of faith and a call to defend that faith whatever the consequences.

M. Night Shyamalan's *Signs* puts yet another face on the conflict faith can breed in men. Mysterious crop signs appear in the cornfield beside the house of Reverend Graham Hess (Mel Gibson), an Episcopalian priest. As Hess tries to discern how a five hundred foot circle of corn could be so perfectly flattened, we come to know him as a man who lost his faith after the death of his wife in an automobile accident. On a wall in the house is an imprint where a cross once hung, and he tells several neighbors to stop calling him "Reverend." When Hess and his family know for certain that aliens have invaded the planet and that some are near the house, they prepare a final lavish supper. But at that meal Hess upsets his children and his brother by refusing to say grace. "I'm not wasting another minute of my life on prayer," he says. "Not one more minute."

At one point, Hess and his brother Merrill (Joaquin Phoenix) are seated together on a sofa after putting Hess's children to bed. Merrill wishes aloud that his brother could again believe in God. In a response that deserves to be quoted in full, Hess gives us the philosophical heart of *Signs*:

"People break down into two groups. When they experience something lucky, group number one sees it as more than luck, more than coincidence. They see it as a sign, evidence, that there is someone up there, watching out for them. Group number two sees it as just pure luck. Just a happy turn of chance. I'm sure the people in group number two are looking at those fourteen lights in a very suspicious way. For them, the situation is a fifty-fifty. Could be bad, could be good. But deep down, they feel that whatever happens, they're on their own. And that fills them with fear. Yeah, there are those people. But there's a whole lot of people in group number one. When they see those fourteen lights, they're looking at a miracle. And deep down, they feel that whatever's going to happen, there will be someone there to help them. And that fills them with hope. See, what you have to ask yourself is what kind of person are you? Are you the kind that sees signs, that sees miracles? Or do you believe that people just get lucky? Or, look at the questions this way: Is it possible that there are no coincidences?"

Merrill decides that he belongs with those who feel "there will be someone to help them" and is comforted by this realization. His brother Graham, however, puts himself squarely in the other group and declares to Merrill that they are alone and must decide for themselves how to live their lives.

After Graham's son miraculously survives an attack by one of the aliens and the enemy has left the planet, Graham recovers his lost faith. In the last scene of the movie, the cross is again on the wall, and Graham is putting on his priestly collar, a doubter now restored to belief, ready to go into the world again as Christ's representative, a richer and wiser man than the broken creature encountered in the beginning of the film.

Part V

Character Is Destiny: Mentoring, Males, and Motion Pictures

He's giving them his 'what every boy needs to hear about being a man' speech. A lot of men have heard that speech over the years. A lot of men.

—*Secondhand Lions*

Men Making Men

Sometimes we meet another man who needs our help—a son struggling with college, a thirty-something who believes his life has
lost its purpose, a middle-aged man trying to bring flames to the
embers of his marriage. We reach out to assist and encourage those who
have lost their way, but may find ourselves feeling useless when we try to
lend them a hand, like guides who have misplaced their map and com-
pass. We parents, we mentors, we teachers and coaches discover we lack
the inspiration and knowledge needed to give of ourselves.

This need for direction in our efforts can present many problems.
The father of two young sons who himself grew up fatherless may flail
about looking for ways to impart lessons to his children, unsure of what
it means to be a father or how to pass along what he does know. A coach
may know how to teach basketball fundamentals to a troubled teenager,
but not the fundamentals of life. A teacher pushes his students to excel,
but is puzzled by the superior performance of his female students when
compared to that of the males and finds himself at a loss as to how to
bridge this gap.

We have already reviewed elsewhere in this book some of the reasons behind this dilemma: divorce, absentee fathers, the neglect of
young men by society, the twisted views of manhood presented in television and movies, the raising up of rock stars and athletes as heroes for

male emulation, the feminization of men as seen in fashion magazines and on television, and perhaps most importantly, a sense among young males that they are increasingly irrelevant both to society and to family. Given the fact that this diminution of manhood has taken place over several decades, mentors and parents may lack the skills and knowledge needed to pass along lessons to the males in their charge.

Of course, the most effective means of teaching the young wisdom, courage, and virtue is by daily example. The father who drinks too much, who abuses his wife, who falters in his duties regarding his work, is, whether he knows it or not, teaching lessons to his children. The coach intent on winning games teaches his players that victory is more important than sportsmanship and honor. The executive who drives himself hard and performs well on the job but who lies to his superiors or cheats on his wife is sending a message to his subordinates. Indeed, men anywhere charged with responsibility—from the foreman of a construction crew to the pastor of a church—are closely observed by the younger men working with them, and will be found worthy or wanting of emulation depending on their behavior.

In our fretful and therapeutic society, some of the apprehensions about raising good men are unfounded. The mother who is alone responsible for the training of her children may well know in her heart what a good man is and will seek adult role models for her son and even for her daughter, so that the young woman will herself come to know what should be valued in men. Like other parents, this mother will understand that boys and girls, despite the denials of some ivory-tower sociologists, really do pursue different interests and approach problems from different directions, and that these differences in gender require insight and empathy. To mark accurately what young men not only need but also at some level want—to grow into a manhood embracing the ancient virtues of courage, wisdom, justice, and temperance—is to move instinctively toward helping them, however clumsily, attain those goals.

In providing models for young men, however, we parents and mentors may need models of our own. How, we may ask ourselves, can I best inspire those in my charge? How can I as a parent or mentor help a young man work his way into manhood without misleading him or suppressing worthy ambitions and desires? Where can I discover models to guide or inspire my own teaching?

Once again Hollywood can help us with this search. Some films—John Wayne's *The Cowboys* or the education of Luke Skywalker in the *Star Wars* movies—are classics in mentorship. Such movies overtly address the teaching of the young from the standpoint of the mentors themselves. In *The Cowboys*, for example, John Wayne plays a cattleman in the Old West who must take his herd to market, but whose men desert him. He hires on a crew of boys who, on their first cattle drive, become men through a series of tests the trail throws at them: bad weather, bad men, the physical rigor of rising before dawn each day to do a man's work. Just as importantly, they watch Wayne and learn from him the lessons of courage, grit, and sacrifice.

Other films are less well known in terms of this theme, but deserve our attention for the lessons taught. In *Gran Torino*, Walt Kowalski (Clint Eastwood), a retired Detroit autoworker mourning the death of his wife, becomes involved with his Hmong neighbors after a local gang threatens them. (During the Vietnam War the Hmong were an ethnic group in South Vietnam who supported the United States.) Although Kowalski at first despises many of his neighbors, eventually he takes the young Thao Vang Lor (Bee Vang) under his tutelage, teaching him how to engage in barbershop banter and showing him the value of tools and hard work. When giving Thao some of his tools, Kowalski tells him: "Take these three items, some WD-40, a vice grip, and a roll of duct tape. Any man worth his salt can fix almost any problem with this stuff alone."

Kowalski's words are both humorous and ironic. The viewer knows that the problems of the neighborhood won't be fixed by duct tape or a squirt of WD-40. Yet these gifts and the examples that accompany them—Kowalski taking care of his lawn, his house, and his prized Gran Torino, defending his home against the punks who make life miserable on the streets—are precisely what Thao needs to witness to begin his own journey to manhood. "You hang out with him," Thao's sister tells Kowalski. "You teach him to fix things…And you're a better man than our own father was. You're a good man."

Though the relationship between Kowalski and Thao Vang Lor is secondary to the larger theme of the movie, Eastwood gives a fine performance of a man who, having failed as a father to his own sons, redeems himself by sharing his knowledge of tools and his values of manhood with a young immigrant.

We see a similar generosity toward the young in *Master and Commander*, where the HMS Surprise battles the French ship, the Acheron, during the Napoleonic Wars. Captain Jack Aubrey (Russell Crowe) teaches the young midshipmen on his vessel the art of navigation, instructs them in the deeds and follies of the men who came before them, reprimands them when they make mistakes, and serves as their example in his practice of courage, cunning, and the dispensation of justice. By his words and actions, Aubrey reminds both his crew and filmgoers that not all teaching takes place in a classroom, that such mentoring occurs during the performance of daily tasks and duties.

Aubrey himself is aware of the debt he owes to his own mentors, the captains, particularly Lord Nelson, under whom he once served, the men who taught him the skills he now passes on to others. Over supper one evening, when a midshipman asks for an anecdote about Lord Nelson, Aubrey tells him of a famous incident in which Nelson revealed his patriotism. During a cold night, Nelson refused the offer of a cloak, saying that his "zeal for king and country" kept him warm. "I know it sounds absurd," Aubrey tells the officers gathered at the table, "and were it from any other man, you'd cry out, 'Oh, what pitiful stuff,' and dismiss it as mere enthusiasm. But with Nelson…you felt your heart glow."

Aubrey also reminds us that not all lessons need be spoken. At one point, as mentioned earlier in this book, Aubrey makes a present of a biography of Lord Nelson to a young midshipman, Blakeney (Max Pirkis), who has lost an arm during battle aboard the ship. When Aubrey leaves, we see the boy open the book to the first page, where a picture of Nelson with only one arm looks out at us. The silent lesson Aubrey has given the boy is clear: the loss of your limb is not the end of your life.

In *Finding Forrester*, William Forrester (Sean Connery) plays a reclusive writer who reluctantly takes a young black man, Jamal Wallace (Rob Brown) under his wing. Like Kowalski and Aubrey, Forrester first connects with his young pupil through his dominance and the teaching of practicalities, in this case certain techniques in writing. Like the others, Forrester also instructs Jamal in the ways of the world. The scene in which he advises Jamal on how to please a woman—"The key to a woman's heart is an unexpected gift at an unexpected time"—is alone worth the price of a ticket to this movie.

Despite his role as mentor, however, William Forrester himself is mired in the adolescent stage of his manhood. For decades, he has hidden out in the apartment, angry with his critics and avoiding contact with people. He has taken no risks, found little outside his apartment to love, and lived an uncommitted life. Devastated long ago by his beloved brother's death, followed swiftly by the deaths of his parents, Forrester has turned his back on the world, affection, and friendship. Though Jamal learns much about literature, writing, and life from the older man, they eventually reverse roles, with Jamal guiding Forrester back into a world of people and their problems. This situation reminds us that parents and mentors often learn lessons themselves while teaching.

In *Dead Poets Society*, John Keating (Robin Williams), a newly hired English professor at an exclusive school for boys, attempts by unconventional means to instill a love of poetry in his students. Despite his occasional descent into histrionics, Keating reveals to us a textbook method of mentoring the young. He makes us see that we must touch the hearts of those we wish to teach. Knowing that poetry and Shakespeare do not automatically enliven the passions of seventeen-year-old males, Keating understands he must seize the attention of his pupils by bringing poetry to life. He is passionate, loves what he teaches, and recognizes that the young appreciate drama, humor, and idealism. During one classroom scene, Keating has the boys huddle around him and says:

We don't read and write poetry because it's cute. We read and write poetry because we are members of the human race, and the human race is filled with passion. And medicine, law, business, engineering, these are noble pursuits and necessary to sustain life. But poetry, beauty, romance, love, these are what we stay alive for.

On another occasion, Keating orders the students to rip out a part of their texts in which the author has attempted near-mathematical comparisons of poetry. He tells the boys: "This is a battle, a war, and the casualties could be your hearts and souls."

Keating's attempts to reach students, even those oriented primarily toward mathematics and the sciences, reveal a vision of manhood he wants to share with his pupils. Fully human men, he implicitly says, feel as well as think, contemplate as well as act. The mind of an engineer need not preclude the soul of a poet.

For teachers and mentors, fathers, brothers, and friends, *Dead Poets Society* also reminds us that our best teaching efforts may end in failure, even ruins. Becoming a man is difficult, and so is helping adolescents. We have no guarantees of success when we teach the young, when we guide them, when we help them fulfill their destiny. Falsely accused of encouraging a student to disobey his father, a rebellion that ends in the young man's suicide, John Keating is dismissed in disgrace from his teaching post. Yet Keating's greatest failure lies not in the death of Neil Perry (Robert Sean Leonard), but with another student, Richard Cameron (Dylan Kussman), who has rejected the lessons of manhood taught by Keating. Most of the boys honor Keating as he leaves the classroom and the school by standing in silent tribute on their desks, despite the shouted threats of the school's headmaster. Cameron remains seated. With him, Keating has failed in his mission.

In *The Emperor's Club*, which we reviewed earlier, William Hundert (Kevin Kline) teaches classical history and philosophy to high school students. Here, too, is a vivid portrait of a mentor. Less eccentric than Keating, and certainly more stoic in the face of adversity, Hundert cares about his students, wants to see them grow into manhood, and uses the classics to give them a boost into the saddle. In a voice-over at the beginning of the film, Hundert says: "As I've gotten older, I realize I'm certain of two things. Days that begin with rowing on a lake are better than days that do not. Second, a man's character is his fate."

As we saw earlier in this book, Hundert fails in his efforts to help form the character of Sedgewick Bell (Emile Hirsch), the spoiled, surly son of a wealthy senator. When he visits Senator Bell, Sedgewick's father, to discuss Sedgewick's deficiencies, their conversation ends abruptly over this issue:

Mr. Hundert: Sir, it is my job to mold your son's character, and if….

Senator Bell: Mold him? Jesus God in heaven, son, you're not gonna mold my boy. Your job is to teach my son. You teach him his times tables. Teach him why the world is round. Teach him who killed who and when and where. That is your job. You, sir, will not mold my son. I will mold him.

And mold him the senator does. As previously stated, Bell goes on to become as corrupt and as cynical as his father.

Yet Hundert remains hopeful. In spite of his failures, he keeps his vision of the true and the good, striving always to bring these ideals into the classroom. He still believes that a man's character is his fate. "However much we stumble," he says in another voice-over, "it is a teacher's burden always to hope that with learning a boy's character might be changed. And so, the destiny of a man."

All parents and mentors have a right to that same hope. We must enter the battle believing we can make a difference, but always with the understanding that victory is not guaranteed.

Dangerous Waters

More than any generation in history, we are concerned with the protection of our adolescents. We coddle children, trying to parry every blow that may come their way. We yank seesaws and slides from playgrounds, and diving boards from swimming pools. We root through bags of candy at Halloween, looking for poison and razor blades, despite the fact that in fifty years no neighbor has poisoned a child during these festivities. As these children become teenagers, we teach them about sex, with some advocating the need for protection in the form of condoms and pills, though we often fail to teach them how to protect their hearts. Even those who preach purity and chastity surround their teens with television, the internet, and cell phones, allowing them access to all the temptations offered by these devices. We lecture our teens on the dangers of drugs and alcohol, and then send them off on poorly chaperoned high school trips.

Yet we rarely question the sexual mores and images of our society, the advertisements, television shows, and movies, the pornography on the internet, all those slick lies designed to make whores of our women and rakes of our men. Those who do tell young men to honor their bodies and to respect women, to treat them as persons rather than as objects, usually find themselves lone voices in a sexual wilderness, competing in a jungle filled with images of women for whom respect is a foreign word.

These circumstances bring special difficulties to non-parental mentors. Teachers, pastors, Scout leaders, Big Brothers, coaches, and indeed anyone who guides young people understand the attendant dangers of such work today, chief of which is the possibility of being accused of sexual molestation. Unfounded accusations of molestation can permanently damage a mentor's reputation.

Mentors would be wise to follow the guidelines of those organizations—the Boy Scouts, for example, or the Catholic Church—that have already faced these difficulties with some of their own adult leaders. The most basic rule of these guidelines is this: unless in a public place, never allow yourself to be alone with the young person you are mentoring. This simple self-imposed regulation lies at the basis of any safety guidelines for mentoring.

In one movie in particular, Hollywood teaches a lesson about the dangers and difficulties of mentoring young men. This movie is Mel Gibson's *The Man Without A Face*, which introduces viewers to twelve-year-old Charles E. "Chuck" Norstadt (Nick Stahl), a boy who is fighting a war on two fronts. He is desperate to enter the military academy once attended by his deceased father, but must pass a battery of difficult academic tests to gain admission. He has the desire to study, but lacks any clear direction. In addition, he must battle two women in his life: his mother Catherine (Margaret Whitton) and his angry older sister (Fay Masterson). His mother is dating a university professor, but he is a buffoon spouting liberal pieties. Chuck is desperately in need of a strong man in his life.

Enter Justin McLeod (Mel Gibson). Scarred with burns on the right side of his body and face, McLeod, whom the teenagers of the town call "Hamburger Head" and "The Freak," was once a teacher. When Chuck finds this out, he summons up his courage and asks McLeod to tutor him in Latin, poetry, writing, and math. Though in the beginning McLeod vehemently refuses, he eventually relents and begins working Chuck hard, both physically and mentally. When Chuck bucks up against such a regimen, McLeod throws a Latin phrase at him—"*Aut disce aut discede,*" meaning "Either learn or leave." He is the "tough-love" man whom Chuck needs.

As Chuck—or Norstadt, as McLeod calls him—grows closer to his teacher, we learn more about McLeod's accident. He suffered the burns in a car accident while driving a pupil home from a debate tournament. The young man died in the accident, and in the wake of the tragedy McLeod was accused of having an improper relationship with his pupil. Forced to resign his teaching post, he has retreated to this small coastal town in Maine to live alone and aloof from others.

This movie, Gibson's directorial debut, offers valuable instruction in mentorship, forcefully demonstrating the need in our young men's lives for strong male role models. Catherine's lover is a poor role model, a walking cliché of a hip professor who offers Chuck little in the way of help or direction. His older sister's boyfriend weakly defends Chuck against the verbal attacks of his sister. Only in McLeod does Chuck find a man who demands much of him, who abides by a code, who has strength and a sense of honor and purpose.

McLeod's house reinforces this masculine ideal. The furniture is dark and heavy, the walls lined with books, paintings, photographs, busts, records. By contrast, Chuck's home seems sterile, a middle-class beach house of 1968. It offers no comforts for Chuck. His family lacks discipline and structure; they share no meals together, and when they do come into contact with one another, the collision most often results in anger and shouting.

The Man Without A Face also gives viewers a good hard look at the dangers of mentoring. After an argument with his sister, during which she reveals that Chuck's father was not an Air Force pilot but a drunk and a schizophrenic, Chuck flees his home, goes to McLeod, and spends the night in his house. After Catherine and the police accuse McLeod of sexual desires for Chuck, he and the boy are forbidden to see each other. (Note well: in the novel by Isabelle Holland on which the movie is based, the relationship between man and boy is much more ambiguous.)

Given the accusations of McLeod's past, I found this part of the movie somewhat unbelievable. Why would an honorable man like McLeod allow Chuck to spend the night at his house? Mentors must always be aware of propriety, of how their relationship to the young men under their direction may look to outsiders. As stated above, the wise mentor will meet with his student only in public places or in the presence of another adult. Never will he say or do anything that might be taken amiss by the young man in his charge or by other observers.

Finally, *The Man Without A Face* offers some mixed comments on masculinity in general. The year is 1968, that awful year of upheaval and change in America, a time when the old ideas of masculinity and their attendant positive qualities—strength, honor, duty—were under heavy fire. It is ironic that Chuck, so desperate to flee his household of women, wants to go to military school during the Vietnam era. At one point, Chuck drifts through a cocktail party hosted by his mother. Another guest teases Chuck about his military ambitions. The professor, who is a little drunk, breaks into the conversation.

Professor: You know this whole Air Force bit is something that Chuck's just into for the moment. Once he understands what the Pentagon is really doing over there in Vietnam...I'm just glad he's way too young for the draft.

Chuck (slowly rising from the sofa and looking directly at the professor): You know, actually there's nothing I can think of that I'd rather do than drop napalm for a living.

In sharp contrast to these characters, McLeod walks and moves like a man with purpose. He confronts Chuck when he plagiarizes an essay. He offers advice when Chuck asks for it. He seeks to inspire Chuck to go beyond his limitations, to push him into pushing himself.

And here we come to another danger that goes along with teaching and guiding our young people. Faced with the task of helping boys become men, men and women must offer challenges leading to that goal.

They must have high expectations. Whether the student is as young as Chuck or is a twenty-five year-old still trying to reach his potential as a man, the parent or teacher must do as McLeod does. Demands must be made, goals set, challenges created. No other adult in Chuck's life is offering those challenges; no one but McLeod sets him on this path.

High expectations lead to high performance. A young man seeking to improve his basketball game needs a demanding coach. A man who has fallen on his face through drink, drugs, bankruptcy, divorce or other such calamities needs a tough-minded mentor who will help him make his way back into the world. Whatever style of teaching or coaching a mentor practices, he must be willing to raise the bar and then insist that his young man leap over that bar.

High expectations lead to high performance.

A Night at the Movies

Long ago, I taught for two years as an instructor in Adult Basic Education at a state prison in Hazelwood, North Carolina. The educational levels of the prisoners in my classroom ranged from second grade to high school. About every two months, both for academic and entertainment purposes, I showed a movie to these students. Our class itself lasted about two hours, so I ran movies less than 100 minutes in length, thereby allowing at least some small amount of time for discussion.

The discussion and the reaction of the prisoners after a showing of *Zulu* were memorable. As we have already seen, this movie tells the story of the fighting in 1879 between the Zulu and British troops at Rorke's Drift. In the film, as in the real battle, both sides fight bravely; the British win because of their superb discipline and their expert marksmanship with their Martini-Henry rifles.

The movie prompted some excellent discussion. Mike, a black man who that year earned his GED and later became a welder, stoutly—and correctly—asserted that the Zulu would have won had they been better marksman with the rifles they'd captured earlier at the Battle of Iswalanda. Others in the class, which was equally divided between blacks and whites, debated the meaning of courage and what it might take to charge the British mealy-bag walls, as the Zulu did, or to resist that charge, as the British did. This lively discussion, laced with jokes and some profanity, impressed me, rousing my awareness of the value of movies as a teaching tool.

While writing *Movies Make the Man*, I decided to offer a movie night for young men. To achieve success, careful preparation seemed in order. The selection of viewers was, I thought, key to a good discussion. Simply to gather a dozen acquaintances to watch a movie might produce some interesting results, but such a hit-and-miss arrangement possessed risks and disadvantages, chiefly the possible failure to generate any discussion at all. It struck me that men with a common bond—my prisoners, for example—would almost certainly be more open to discussion than a collection of casual friends.

I therefore chose as guinea pigs for my experiment students from my homeschooling seminars and their fathers. I limited the group to twelve, but only ten were able to attend. A physician brought his two older sons. An attorney attended, along with one of his sons, a freshman in college. The last outsider was a salesman who frequently traveled abroad and his son, age fifteen. Completing our circle were two of my sons, one a sophomore in high school and the other an attorney, age twenty-four, who had just completed his first year of practice.

All four families had similar backgrounds. All were conservative or libertarian in their politics. All the high-school students were being educated at home. In each family, religious faith—there were two Presbyterian families and two Catholic families—served as a foundation for living.

The movie I also chose with some care. I wanted it to appeal to fifteen year olds as well as to the adult men, and it needed to be short and preeminently discussable. *Master and Commander* was my first choice, but it runs too long. Finally, I settled on *Groundhog Day*, which we looked at earlier. This movie runs around 100 minutes and throws up many points for analysis.

To deepen a feeling of camaraderie and so enhance our discussion, I served a light, simple supper: chicken wings, a vegetable tray, chips of various kinds, salsa, and fruit. For dessert one of the men brought brownies, a gift from his wife.

We spent about forty-five minutes eating and visiting, and then began the business at hand. To let the others see what I intended by watching the movie, I read them part of the preface to this book, then in rough draft, and played the movie. Of those watching, only the four teenagers had not previously seen *Groundhog Day*. (Note: Do not be afraid to show a movie for discussion others have seen. We are so accustomed to electronic fare—movies, television, the internet—that we rarely go below the surface when watching a screen. In fact, it may even help the discussion if the audience has previously viewed the film.)

Groundhog Day was a hit. There was a good deal of laughter as Phil tries to come to grips with his peculiar form of immortality. Having watched this movie myself only three days earlier, I observed the laughter of the others and found that even I, who had watched the movie so many times, enjoyed it more in company than I had alone.

Our discussion of *Groundhog Day* began slowly, but increased its pace as my guests realized that the parameters to the discussion were few and vague. There were, in other words, no right answers, no specific direction we needed to take. I wanted to discuss the movie in terms of virtue and manhood, but even more I hoped it would serve as jumping-off place to different topics.

This is indeed what happened. Our talk ranged from the nature of time in the movie to the importance of using our own time wisely, from the growing affection of Phil for Rita to the meaning of love and marriage in general, from the movie's depiction of spirituality to the reminiscences by the adults about the lack of faith in their own younger years.

The dads and two of the young men—Jake, my eldest son, and Christopher, the college freshman—carried the discussion. From my years of teaching, I had expected this development, which was one reason I had chosen articulate adults to join me. If you decide to lead such a group, keep in mind that many teens may say little or nothing during the conversation. This reticence stems not from their inability to think or to digest the movie—on the contrary, most of them will be thinking furiously during the discussion—but from a shyness of their years, a fear of speaking out, and an inability to articulate arguments. These barriers to discussion are normal in teenagers, and they should not be pushed too hard to make a contribution. Hosts for a movie night therefore need to be sure there are on hand adults or young people who will freely discuss the film. Those who are silent are nonetheless learning about the movies, about manhood, and about themselves.

Discussing movies in this way can also lead to *seeing* the movie. All of us, as I stated above, watch movies and television shows, but few of us actually *see* them. We tend to skim the surface. As all of those who had previously seen *Groundhog Day* agreed, they had watched the movie the first time for enjoyment, but had taken little away with them from the film. All of them only remembered the movie as "some guy repeating his day over and over again."

Watching a movie with a purpose is like living with a purpose. We take away far more from the experience when we watch with intent. Inundated by movies and television, we forget that the men and women who write the stories and direct the action intend, however basely, a moral. Often they employ symbols to drive home their themes and use gesture, word, and action for a purpose. All too often, dulled viewers take home only the plot of the film and so miss the great pleasure and learning that come with careful attention.

Although I had watched this movie perhaps six or seven times, the discussion deepened my own thoughts about the film. Josiah and Richard, for example, pointed out that Phil's job as a weathercaster meant he is in some sense a prognosticator, a foreteller of future events. His repetition of days, his ability to predict each moment, eventually help lead him to redemption. Both the physician, Tom, and my son Jake related that their wives disliked the movie. Tom's wife remembered it as showing how men manipulated women, which is true for the first three quarters of the film. Rita despises Phil for his sleazy attempts to woo her. By the end of the movie, however, Phil has become attractive to Rita. All his conniving and scheming vanish, replaced instead by accomplishments—he learns to speak French and Italian, reads poetry, and plays the piano. Most importantly, she is drawn to him by his practice of virtue rather than vice. (It occurred to me that showing *Groundhog Day* to a group of women and their daughters might be highly instructive in regard to the differences between men and women.)

Our discussion covered a lot of territory. Richard thought aloud about his father-in-law who was sharing his home, an eighty-year-old suffering from dementia who had worked thirty years as a paper cutter. Because of his dementia, this man often repeated his days like Phil, but he had lived his life as a devout Christian and so carried his faith and compassion into the recreation center where he spent some days of his week. The discussion then moved to the importance of habit in developing a virtue. Tom spoke at length about the need for young people to set goals for themselves, goals larger than going to college, getting a good job, marrying the right women, buying a large house. He pointed out the disturbing number of suicides among young people, and talked at length about how the lack of a purpose in life has damaged so many men and women.

Our discussion, incidentally, soon developed to the point where my own comments and questions as a moderator proved unnecessary. About forty-five minutes into the discussion, I quietly left the room for a few minutes to test whether the discussion might continue without me. When I returned, the conversation regarding the movie and life had not slackened.

Perhaps the best indication of the success of the evening occurred as we were breaking up, when several of the participants suggested more movie nights. Jeremy, my fifteen-year-old, envisioned a group that might meet once a month in different homes to watch and discuss other films.

Failure is a possibility in such an endeavor. In addition to the planning mentioned above, the leader of the group may find that he has to ask specific questions to get a discussion started. He may also find himself having to push for a deeper look into the movie. This is his job; after all, he has selected the movie and its audience.

One final note: despite the commonalities among these fathers and sons—their race, levels of education, and most importantly, their religious backgrounds—the words "manhood" and "manliness" seemed to bring with it a tentativeness, an awkwardness, among both men and boys that evening. This in turn seems to bear out what was stated in the beginning chapters of *Movies Make the Man*, that the idea of manhood has undergone so many attacks and so much abuse that men themselves feel awkward with the term. It is difficult to imagine women shying away from words like "feminine" or "womanhood."

Here then is one more reason for men to inspire in the young the desire to know what it means to be a man in our postmodern world. We must not allow social engineers or cultural dictators to put us into some sort of box defining manhood or take away altogether our ideas of manliness. Instead, we must each seek our own ideal, to find and to live out the real meaning of the place of manhood in our families, in our society, and especially in ourselves.

Parting Notes

So what have we learned here?

We have seen that many movies can give us a strong sense of the meaning of manhood. These movies, and many others, teach us that men can be both tender and tough, that endurance and grit matter, that the best of men assume their share of responsibility toward their families and others around them, that the ancient virtues—justice, courage, wisdom, temperance—remain the coinage of manhood.

Of course, we must always remember that Hollywood is a storytelling machine. For the sake of story and drama, writers and directors simplify the complexities of real life and real situations. Two hours of screen time leave little room for showing the humdrum details and repetitive motions making up the bulk of our lives. In *Hoosiers*, for example, we do not see the alcoholic assistant coach Shooter drinking his way through the evenings, gathering firewood, and making meals from beans and bread. In thirty seconds, the director creates Shooter in our minds. Moreover, few of us will find ourselves battling for a heavyweight championship like Rocky Balboa or being visited by a guardian angel like George Bailey in *It's A Wonderful Life*.

Life is more complicated than a movie. Life is also much more of an adventure. Most of us fail to appreciate the adventure we live, the miracles surrounding us. Too often we lack the ability to stand outside ourselves, to see the big picture. We dwell in the particular and familiar, caught up in our own web of tragedy and comedy, joy and despair, and so fail to comprehend fully that most remarkable of pilgrimages—our own lives.

Yet even here Hollywood can lend us the lens needed to see ourselves more clearly. The pre-med student facing failure in his organic chemistry class faces the same temptation to cheat as the young professor in *Quiz Show*. The father breaking his back sixty hours a week to feed his family faces the same formidable challenges as James J. Braddock in *Cinderella Man*.

Confronted by the demands of living, mature men know how to handle themselves. Like the movie heroes presented here, these men live by a code. They don't fumble about looking for the easy way out or the dishonest angle. They know the final cost of such options, the price exacted when they fail to abide by their code. They know that reading books, watching movies, and listening to the wisdom of others are only the beginning of the journey, that they must daily face their moments of truth.

In the preceding pages, we have neglected one by-product of living as a man. This is the satisfaction, amounting to a deep interior joy, which is produced, as Robert E. Lee once wrote, "from duty faithfully performed." The virtuous man who struggles against the odds, who bends but does not break, will find this joy. At the end of his day—yes, and at the end of his life—this man can say to himself: "I was here. I have lived as a man should live. I have born the brunt of battle. I have run the race. I have loved, bled, sweated, wept, and laughed.

"I was here."

Appendix

Blast From The Past

In the beginning of *Movies Make The Man*, I explained why I had deliberately ignored action movies and foreign films. Many of these, as I mentioned, offer a means of discussion and growth, and should not be neglected. Other movies, particularly older films, didn't make the cut here because of space limitations.

Below is a list of ten of these movies that may stimulate discussions of manhood.

Angels With Dirty Faces—Michael Curtiz's tale of two boyhood friends from a rough neighborhood. One becomes a priest, the other a criminal. Those new to James Cagney may want to check out *White Heat* after this introduction.

The Ghost And Mrs. Muir—Rex Harrison as a fiery sea captain—and ghost—stands in stark contrast to the bounder who pursues Mrs. Muir. Another film in which the writers contrast two visions of manhood.

Glory—An excellent Civil War film about racial prejudice, manhood, and courage. Matthew Broderick, Morgan Freeman, and Denzel Washington give solid performances in this true story about a black

Massachusetts regiment and its doomed attack on Confederate fortifications.

Gone With The Wind—With Scarlett O'Hara as the centerpiece, Victor Fleming's classic masterpiece may strike you as an odd choice for this list, but the two main male characters—Ashley Wilkes and Rhett Butler—offer a nuanced contrast in male virtues. How do we react if our country goes to war? More importantly, how do we cope if we are defeated?

Robin Hood—This older film, starring Errol Flynn, should be watched for Flynn's depiction of Robin Hood. In so many movies, men are depicted as grim, resigned, serious. Flynn's Robin Hood takes enormous delight in being alive in the moment, taking pleasure in everything from eating one of the king's deer to battling the king's men. Here is a reminder of joy and exuberance in living.

The Lord Of The Rings Trilogy—Treachery, loyalty, duty, love, friendship, greed: these movies about Hobbits, Elves, Dwarves, and the other inhabitants of Middle Earth provide the food for great discussions.

The Man Who Shot Liberty Valence—This movie raises Pilate's question of Christ: "What is truth?" Do we go for the legend or the truth? John Wayne gives us a man who for all his strength and character still suffers the loss of a woman he loves to a man whose life he has saved.

My Fair Lady—Many young men gag at musicals, but this one deserves a look. Rex Harrison as Professor Higgins and Audrey Hepburn as Eliza clash in this adaptation of Shaw's classic battle of the sexes. In contrast with many other books and films, *My Fair Lady* offers the unusual story of a man transforming the character and behavior of a woman. An excellent film on the nature of relationships and love.

My Favorite Year—In this comedy, Peter O'Toole gives us a character built from his own life and from that of Errol Flynn. He plays an aging, drunken movie star who must appear on television in the 1950s, when shows were often shot live. Excellent for its depiction of fame and of a man who must finally come to terms with the façade he has spent decades constructing.

Spartacus—Called by some the greatest guy movie ever made, Stanley Kubrick's study in oppression, rebellion, and justice can't compete with the technology of *Gladiator*, but it remains a classic. The real story of Spartacus, the slave who grew an army from 80 gladiators to 90,000 escaped slaves, is as good as the movie.

Prompts For Discussion

1. What virtues did the main character display? Was he brave? Decisive? Kind? Intelligent? Do you consider yourself virtuous? If so, what does that mean to you?

2. What are the main character's flaws? Does he address these flaws in the movie? Is he aware of the flaws? What flaws do you see in yourself? Are you able to change these flaws? Or do you need to just accept them in yourself? Can we always see the flaws in ourselves?

3. Does the main character follow any sort of code? Does he fall away from the code? Does he bend the code due to circumstances? Do you have a code that you follow?

4. Does the movie show the main character working at all? What was his attitude toward his job? What is your own attitude toward work?

5. What roles do secondary characters – family, friends, wives, girlfriends – play in the main character's life? What roles do such people play in your life?

6. What crisis or trial did the main character face? What tools – initiative, intelligence, physical strength, and so on – does the main character bring to these trials? What tools do you possess that help you overcome difficulties in your own life?

7. Did the main character change at all over the course of the movie? If so, in what ways? What caused these changes? How difficult is change for you?

8. Select a favorite movie – any movie with a strong male character. Why does the character appeal to you?

9. When asked, two of the young women who helped me edit this book told me what qualities they admired in men. Both first mentioned that they most admired men who respected them as individuals. Other qualities that made their list were intelligence, humor, and authenticity. What qualities do you find attractive in women? What qualities do you possess that women might find attractive in you?

10. Did the movie examine the character's religious beliefs? If so, what were they? How did those beliefs influence the character's virtues or outlook on life? Do you adhere to any beliefs? If so, what impact do they have on your life?

Movies Make The Man:
A List of the Films

Movie	Rating
Blast From the Past	PG-13
Braveheart	R
Bridget Jones' Diary	R
Casablanca	PG
Chariots of Fire	PG
Cinderella Man	PG-13
Cool Hand Luke	PG-13
Crimes and Misdemeanors	PG-13
Das Boot	R
Dead Poets Society	PG
The Emperor's Club	PG-13
Finding Forrester	PG-13
The Fountainhead	Unrated
Gladiator	R
God and Generals	PG-13
The Godfather	R
Good Will Hunting	R

Gran Torino	R
The Great Santini	PG
Groundhog Day	PG
Heaven Knows, Mr. Allison	Unrated
Henry V	PG-13
Hoosiers	PG
It's a Wonderful Life	PG
John Adams	Unrated
Kate and Leop0ld	PG-13
The Last Days of Disco	R
Lilies of the Field	Unrated
Local Color	R
Lonesome Dove	Unrated
A Man For All Seasons	G
The Man Without A Face	PG-13
Master and Commander	PG-13
My Dinner With Andre	PG
On The Waterfront	Unrated
Possession	PG-13
Pride and Prejudice	Unrated
The Pursuit of Happyness	PG-13
A Raisin in the Sun	PG
Quiz Show	PG
Remember the Titans	PG
The Road	R
Rocky II	PG
Rocky	PG
Rocky Balboa	PG
Rumble Fish	R
Saving Private Ryan	R
Secondhand Lions	PG
Sex And The City	R
Shenandoah	PG

Signs	PG-13
Something's Gotta Give	PG-13
Stand and Deliver	PG
Star Trek	PG-13
Tears of the Sun	R
Tender Mercies	PG
The Third Miracle	R
To Kill A Mockingbird	Unrated
True Grit	G
Twelve Angry Men	PG
An Unfinished Life	PG-13
We were Soldiers Once…	
And Young	R
What Women Want	PG-13
Zulu	PG

Made in the USA
Las Vegas, NV
22 May 2024